# The Revolutionary War

D0173446

## The Making of America

# The Revolutionary War

The Chronicle of American History
from 1770 to 1783

**A BLUEWOOD BOOK**

THE MAKING OF AMERICA:
THE REVOLUTIONARY WAR

A Bluewood Book

This edition produced and published in 1996 by
Bluewood Books,
a division of The Siyeh Group, Inc.
38 South B Street, Suite 202
San Mateo, CA 94401

ISBN 0-912517-23-9

Printed in USA

Designed and Edited by Bill Yenne
Design assistant: Azia Yenne
Proofreader: Joan Hayes.

On the cover: A Reenactment of the Battle of
Lexington. *(Photo courtesy of the Massachusetts
office of Trade & Tourism)*

Also in *The Making of America* Series:
*Exploration & Discovery (1492-1606)*
*Our Colonial Period (1607-1770)*

Other titles of interest from
Bluewood Books:

*100 Events That Shaped World History*
*100 Inventions That Shaped World History*
*100 Women Who Shaped World History*
*100 Men Who Shaped World History*
*100 Athletes Who Shaped Sports History*
*100 Folk Heroes Who Shaped World History*
*100 African Americans Who Shaped American History*
*100 Great Cities of World History*
*100 Natural Wonders of the World*
*100 Authors Who Shaped World History*
*100 Explorers Who Shaped World History*

# TABLE OF CONTENTS

# BACKGROUND TO THE REVOLUTION

By the beginning of the 1770s, England's colonies in America had evolved from crude and tenuous outposts, to very complex and prosperous societies. Boston, for example, was more provincial than London, but every bit as sophisticated in terms of society, fashion, culture and higher learning as most other cities in England or continental Europe, if not more so. However, Boston considered itself an English city more than an American city. Most of the colonists from New England to Virginia were thorough Englishmen. They were loyal to the English crown and proud of their origin.

They had a great reverence for English ideas, because they WERE English. English fashions were studiously copied. King George's American subjects were as loyal as those in England itself. The triumph of England over France in 1759 at the climax of the French and Indian War was cheered in the American colonies. The American Englishmen, how-ever, cherished the ideals of right, justice, and liberty, which had been denied to them by the English government. In fact, it was the pursuit of a wider range of social and religious freedom that had brought many of them to America from England. When King George III (1738-1820) refused his American subjects the rights of Englishmen there was trouble, strife, and finally the great American

***BRITAIN'S KING GEORGE III***

Revolution. This marked an epoch not only in the annals of America but in the history of the world.

Despite their sophistication and their location 3,500 miles from England, the colonies belonged to England, and the colonists knew it. The King and Parliament would not concede the same political and commercial rights to them as to England. This was to be a fatal mistake. It led to the passage of trade laws disruptive to the colonists and beneficial to the English.

The theory of colonial government, common among the nations of Europe, gave England a temporary benefit, but ended in disaster. In accord with this policy, the British government planned to give the people in England an advantage, by controlling commerce and industry in the colonies.

To accomplish this, the English passed a series of laws called The Navigation Acts. These stated that certain goods could not be sold or shipped to England. Other goods could be shipped *only* to English ports, and only aboard English or colonial vessels, manned by English or colonial seamen.

In 1673, more restrictions were placed on trade between the colonies. In 1696 a commission was formed in England, called the Lords of the Board of Trade and Plantations to look after the trade relations with the colonies, to make recommendations to colonial governors, and to recommend the veto or approval of laws made by

the colonies. The following year, courts of admiralty were established to try, without a jury, violators of the navigation laws. In 1699 Parliament passed a law prohibiting the colonists, under penalty of a heavy fine, from shipping wool, yarn, woolen manufactures, or any kind of cloth to any colony or jurisdiction outside the colonies proper.

The manufacture of fur hats became an important industry due to the abundancy and relative inexpense. At least 10,000 beaver hats were made annually in New York and New England. Many American merchants invaded the markets of Europe. English manufacturers of felt petitioned Parliament to stop the trade. In 1732, England passed a law which placed a £500 fine on anyone who shipped a fur hat out of the colonies.

The Molasses Act of 1733, placed a high duty on sugar and molasses imported from any place other than the British West Indies. The colonists would have been forced to buy all their sugar and

*ENGLISH TAX STAMPS, CIRCA 1765*

molasses from British merchants and planters; although it was not enforced until 1764. In 1750, Parliament passed a law prohibiting all ironworks and steel foundries in the colonies.

At the expense of the colonies, England tried to build up trade, commerce and industries at home. Some of these laws were not enforced. The colonists either ignored or violated them, inducing smuggling as a big business.

Two generations prior to the reign of George III, England had been ruled chiefly by Parliament. The first two Georges had little to do with the management of the empire and less with that of the colonies.

When George III came to the throne in 1760, he took the reins of government into his own hands. Often had he heard the mandate of his mother ("George, be King!") to behave like a monarch.

It was no easy task to get Parliament to yield to his will. Through monetary bribes and appointment of many members of Parliament and their friends to good offices, he secured control of a majority in Parliament to help him further his schemes.

George III was self-willed, arbitrary, and determined to rule. Among other things, George III decided to try to stop smuggling by enforcing the Navigation Acts. General search warrants called "Writs of Assistance" had been issued to revenue officers. They were authorized to enter any man's house or store at any time to search for smuggled goods.

To enforce the Navigation Acts would have meant a serious loss to the American merchants engaged in shipping. They engaged James Otis, a young but able attorney, to oppose in the English courts, the issuing of these writs. His eloquent and impassioned speeches created enthusiasm in Massachusetts. John Adams was so impressed with Otis' speech that he said, "American independence was then and there born."

George III, who never actually visited his American realm, was oblivious to the subtleties of what went on there. He ruled England and the colonies in his own way; without regard for the wishes of the people. With his bribed Parliament, he soon modified old laws, enacted new ones, and enforced obedience to these laws. This ultimately drove the colonies into union, and later into rebellion.

The colonists had lived for many years far from English royalty and aristocracy. The spirit of freedom and equality had taken a fast hold of them. For years they had practically ruled themselves. They began to look on liberty and freedom as a birthright, and resented any attempt to abridge their rights of self-government.

They were particularly enraged when George Grenville, the prime minister, outlined colonial plans for the King. He proposed to modify the old trade and navigation laws and force obedience to them, and to do so with 10,000 soldiers permanently based in America. Vigorous measures, such as the seizure of ships and cargo, were taken to enforce the old trade and navigation acts. Vessels were stationed along the coasts to watch for smugglers or anyone not complying with the Navigation Acts.

If caught, the smugglers were to be tried by courts of admiralty. The 10,000 soldiers were intended, according to the King, to protect the colonists from the Indians and French. However, one of the motives was to strengthen the King's power and prevent the violation of the revenue laws.

To increase the revenue from the colonies, the 1733 tax on sugar and molasses brought into the colonies was revised in 1764. The new tax law entitled the Stamp Tax, was the straw that broke the back of English rule in Amer-

*COLONISTS IN NEW YORK CITY PROTESTING THE OPPRESSIVE STAMP TAX*

*A POLITICAL CARTOON OF A BRITISH OFFICER QUARTERED IN THE HOME OF A COLONIAL FAMILY*

and Parliament were determined, and proceeded to carry out their plan of taxation.

Over the protest of the Americans, the Stamp Act was passed in March 1765, and scheduled to go into effect on November first. The money raised was to be used in America to support the army; which was, in effect, an army of occupation. The act was a lengthy document

ica. The question of taxation was of prime importance because the King wanted more revenue from the colonies. The tax collected did not yield sufficient funds to pay the officers for collecting it. The quartering of troops in America required money which the colonists were to be coerced to pay.

They opposed paying any tax imposed upon them without their consent. They claimed that they were not represented in Parliament, therefore, Parliament had no right to tax them. "Taxation without representation is tyranny," became their motto.

It was not so much the amount of the tax, as the principle of it. They had already paid in taxes, levied by themselves, more than their share of the expense of the French and Indian War in the 1750s. They were opposed to all direct taxes laid by Parliament, noting that they had exclusive rights to tax.

If the King needed money he should obtain it by a vote of the colonial assemblies, as he formerly had done. The King

stipulating that all bills, notes, bonds, bills of lading, licenses, marriage certificates, and other legal documents should be written or printed on stamped paper made in England.

All pamphlets, almanacs, newspapers and business forms were taxed. The stamps cost from one penny to $50. People obtaining a marriage license, transacting any business, or even buying a newspaper paid a tax. A tax on land, houses, income or any other property is a direct tax, while a tax levied on imports, exports, or the manufacture or sale of products is an indirect tax.

Today, most states have a sales tax levied by and for state government. The Stamp Act was almost unnoticed in England — even in Parliament there was but little discussion — but in America it aroused a storm of violent opposition.

The question was not, "Shall America support the army?" but, "Shall Parliament tax the colonies?"

The colonists were determined not to be taxed except by themselves. They were going to live by the motto, "Taxation without representation is tyranny."

In some towns, people organized themselves into a secret order called "Sons of Liberty," to oppose the Stamp Act.

Public meetings were held to denounce the act. Stamp officers were hung in effigy, and some were forced to resign. Mobs paraded the streets shouting "Liberty, property, and no stamps!" Stamp officers were forced to march in the parade and were made to join in the shouting. Merchants pledged themselves not to import any goods from England until the Stamp Act was repealed. This hurt some English industries, hundreds of people were thrown out of work, business languished, and English merchants petitioned Parliament for the repeal of the Stamp Act.

Ironically, England's loss was America's gain. Manufacturing increased in the colonies because household industries developed to such an extent that each family could produce the chief necessities. Mothers and daughters took up with greater energy the work of weaving and spinning at home and became "Daughters of Liberty."

In Virginia, the House of Burgesses passed a set of resolutions denying the right of Parliament to tax the colonies. Patrick Henry (1736-1799), possibly the greatest of colonial orators, in support of the resolutions, alluded to the tyranny of the King, by saying: "Caesar had his Brutus, Charles I his Cromwell, and George III" — here he paused for a moment for the cry of "Treason! Treason!" raised by several members to cease, then continued — "may profit by

their example. If this be treason, make the most of it."

In Massachusetts, James Otis and Samuel Adams (1722-1803) were stirring the people to open resistance. Plans were formed for a meeting of delegates from all the colonies in New York City. The "Stamp Act Congress," representatives from nine colonies, met on October 7, 1765. The colonies not represented were Virginia, North Carolina, New Hampshire, and Georgia.

After a secret session of 20 days, they prepared a Declaration of Rights and Grievances, which they sent to King George and to both houses of Parliament.

The colonists stated that they had the same allegiance to the crown as Englishmen of the realm; that they were entitled to the same rights as natural-born Englishmen; that Englishmen cannot be taxed except by their own consent; that the colonists were not represented in Parliament; that only representatives of the colonies could tax the colonists; that Parliament could not grant the property of the colonists to the king; that a trial by jury was the inherent right of every British subject in the colony; and that the Stamp Act and other acts (the Sugar Act and Trade Acts) tended to subvert the rights and liberties of the colonists.

When the first of November came, flags were hung at half-mast and bells were muffled and tolled. The colonies were in mourning. Processions carried banners bearing the inscription, "The folly of England and the ruin of America," through the streets.

The colonists did not stop with an expression of grief. There was bitter and

*PATRICK HENRY, SPEAKING BEFORE THE VIRGINIA HOUSE OF BURGESSES IN WILLIAMSBURG, COMPARED KING GEORGE III TO CROMWELL AND BRUTUS.*

violent opposition in most of the colonies. A stamped piece of paper was not to be had. Boxes of stamped paper were seized by mobs and burned. Documents were not legal without stamps, therefore courts were closed and business came to a standstill.

Governors finally issued letters authorizing non-compliance with the law because stamps could not be bought. These difficulties, combined with the cry of distress from the manufacturers in England, led Parliament to repeal the Stamp Act in March 1766. With the repeal of the act, Parliament still insisted

on the right to tax the colonies "in all cases whatsoever."

The colonists had rid themselves of one tax, but it was not long till Charles Townshend, Chancellor of the British Exchequer, brought in a new tax law. The colonists had denied that the King had a right to lay a direct tax, but had admitted that he had a right to lay an indirect tax by placing a duty on imports. In 1767, Parliament passed a new tax law which placed a duty on glass, paper, lead, paints and tea brought into the colonies. The taxes were not heavy, but the money was to be used for a dangerous purpose: to pay the salaries of governors, judges, and other officers, who would thus become entirely independent of the colonial assemblies. In this way the government would be conducted by officials dependent on the King.

By another act the legislature of New York was denied the right to pass any more laws until it complied with the Mutiny Act to furnish quarters and supplies for the soldiers whom the King had sent.

A third Townshend Act created a Board of Commissioners to enforce the laws regulating trade. While building up her monopoly in trade, England was increasing her revenues and attempting to widen and strengthen her rule over the colonies.

The merchants renewed their agreement not to import any more British goods. Ships loaded with such imports were sent back. Individuals pledged themselves not to eat, drink or wear anything imported from England until the duties were removed. Some merchants, prompted by love of money, tried to sell British goods. They were waited on by mobs and their goods destroyed or reshipped. In 1768, the legislature of Massachusetts sent a circular letter, prepared by Samuel Adams to the other colonies urging them to unite and to protect their rights. This enraged the King. His secretary demanded that the assembly withdraw the letter. He asked the governors of the other colonies to prevent their assemblies from taking notice of it. The assemblies disobeyed. They sent protests to Parliament, petitions to the King, and stirred up sentiment in the colonies against the acts. The legislatures of half the colonies were dissolved. It was impossible to enforce the

Townshend Acts without the aid of troops as riots broke out.

Two regiments of soldiers and seven British warships were sent to Boston to strengthen the government. Efforts to enforce the laws brought confrontation. When the revenue officer boarded John Hancock's ship, *LIBERTY*, he was seized and held by a crowd until the cargo of wines was unloaded. The owners forcibly escaped paying the duty. After the officer was released, the British warships seized the *LIBERTY*, because taxes had not been paid on the cargo. A riot followed. The custom house officers were compelled to retreat to their barracks for safety.

England added more fuel to the flame in 1769, when Parliament threatened to revive an old law passed in the sixteenth century reign of Henry VIII: All persons accused of treason were to be shipped to England for trial.

**SAMUEL ADAMS OF MASSACHUSETTS**

# MASSACRE, TEA PARTY AND THE ROAD TO WAR

By 1770, the presence of English troops throughout the American colonies created an atmosphere of tension and distrust. The colonists felt that the last spark of liberty was to be extinguished. No one knew what to expect next. A minor incident might produce a great tragedy.

On the night of March 5, 1770, while a crowd of men and boys were taunting some soldiers in Boston, the troops opened fire — either from panic, fear, or resentment —killing five and wounding six. This event, which has since been known as the Boston Massacre, fanned the passions of the people throughout the colonies and helped to hasten the Revolution.

One night in 1772, colonists with muffled oars rowed to the *Gaspee*, an armed British vessel which had been patrolling the coast of Rhode Island to catch smugglers. They overpowered and bound the crew, took them to the shore, and burned the vessel. These events, along with many others, were bringing matters to a crisis. England made a few feeble attempts to pacify the colonists about a month after the Boston Massacre. Parliament had repealed, the duty on all articles except tea to show that Parliament had a right to tax the colonies.

The King and Parliament had now given up the attempt to tax the colonists for revenue. Their final aim was to uphold the same principle the colonists were opposing. The tax on tea was only threepence a pound, but the colonists refused to import, buy, or drink tea.

Over 17 million pounds of tea accumulated in the warehouses of the East India Company. The company was facing bankruptcy. In desperation, the British government removed the duty of twelvepence a pound, which was paid in England, so that tea could be purchased more cheaply in America than in England. This was a tempting bait, but it did not work.

In 1773, several shiploads of tea were sent to the colonies, with the hope that the people would buy the tea at the low price. The colonists would not even allow the tea to be landed.

In Philadelphia and New York, the people forced the captains of the tea ships to sail back to England. At Annapolis resolute men forced a rich Tory to set fire to his own ship of tea, and in South Carolina the tea was stored in the customhouse for safekeeping.

When the tea ships arrived in Boston, a public meeting was held in Faneuil Hall, "the Cradle of Liberty," as it was called, at which the Tea Tax was denounced. On the night of December 16, 1773, under the leadership of Samuel Adams, a group of men disguised as Mohawk Indians boarded the ships, cut open the tea boxes, and threw the entire cargo of 342 tea chests into the sea. The

incident has since been immortalized in American lore as the Boston Tea Party. The same night, messengers were sent to inform the other towns of what the Boston patriots had done.

The next day Paul Revere (1735-1818), certainly the most famous of revolutionary couriers, set out to carry the message to New York and Philadelphia.

The series of events that culminated in the historic Boston Tea Party enraged George III beyond measure. He concluded that the time to conciliate was past. The hour for punishment had come. He

*FANEUIL HALL IN BOSTON, WHERE THE COLONISTS MET TO PLAN THEIR REVOLT*

*COLONISTS TRASHING TEA CHESTS*

ings people were prohibited from discussing anything but local affairs. Most vestiges of self-government were eliminated. The colonial governor was given the power to send anyone indicted for murder while in the service of the King to England or to another colony for trial. This made officers more active and fearless in using rigorous means to enforce laws. Meanwhile, the Quartering Act legalized the quartering of troops in the colonies. General Thomas Gage (1721-1778), the commander-in-chief of the English army in America was appointed as governor of Massachusetts. Four more regiments of regular troops were placed at his command to enforce the acts and restore order and obedience. If need be, he was ordered to arrest Samuel Adams and John Hancock (1737-1793), the great patriot leaders in Massachusetts, and send them to England for trial. England hoped to be able to starve or coerce Boston and the rest of Massachusetts into obedience.

Boston was not left to fight her battles alone. A wave of sympathy borne by an ocean of indignation swept over the land. South Carolina and Maryland sent corn and rice.

Two important future colonial generals also chipped in. Israel Putnam (1718-1790) drove a flock of sheep from Connecticut to Boston. George Washington (1732-1799) sent £50, and said: "If need be I will raise a thousand people, subsist them at my own expense,

was determined that the "Boston rebels" were to be brought to their senses. Five laws, so severe that they were termed by the colonists "The Intolerable Acts," were passed.

The Boston Port Act closed the port of Boston except to food and fuel. Ships with other cargoes were not allowed to enter or leave the port. British warships were placed there to enforce the act until Boston paid for the tea destroyed. The King was determined to take all power out of the hands of the people of Massachusetts by changing their charter. The King would appoint the governor and members of the council, as well as selecting and dismissing all sheriffs, judges, and magistrates. At town meet-

and march at their head for the relief of Boston."

Virginia legislator Patrick Henry declared in his legendary quote: "We must fight. I repeat it, sir, we must fight. I know not what course others may pursue, but as for me, give me liberty or give me death."

This was the spirit from Maine to Georgia. None of the colonies would stand by and see another crushed into submission by the tyranny of an arbitrary king. The Virginia assembly set aside the day on which the Port Act was to go into effect, as a day of "fasting, humiliation and prayer." The governor dismissed the assembly. Its members met again and appointed a committee to correspond with the other colonies for the purpose of calling a meeting of delegates from all the colonies. The place selected for the meeting was Philadelphia. The body which met there would be called the First Continental Congress.

*THE VIEW FROM SHORE OF THE BOSTON TEA PARTY ON DECEMBER 16, 1773*

# THE FIRST CONTINENTAL CONGRESS

The delegates to the First Continental Congress met in Philadelphia on September 5, 1774. Forty-five persons were present, representing every colony but Georgia, where the governor prevented the choice of delegates. Among the leading figures present were Patrick Henry, Richard Henry Lee and George Washington of Virginia; Samuel Adams and John Adams of Massachusetts; John Dickinson of Pennsylvania; Roger Sherman of Connecticut; and John Rutledge of South Carolina. The Congress continued in session until October 26, endorsing the conduct of the people of Boston, and urging them to stand firm.

The Continental Congress asked the people of the colonies to unite in support of Massachusetts. They resolved not to use or import any British goods or products until the liberties of the colonies were secured.

Congress sent a petition to the King, asking for a "redress of grievances" and issued a remarkable paper known as the "Declaration of Resolves," which the colonists accepted as an expression of ideals wished for and hopes to be attained. Among other things that the Congress asserted were:

1. The right to life, liberty, and property.

2. That they were entitled to the rights of Englishmen and all other rights promised in the colonial charters.

3. That they alone had the right to tax themselves.

4, That they had the right to peaceably assemble and petition the King and Parliament for a redress of grievances.

5. That the keeping of a standing army in the colonies in time of peace was against all law.

These rights, they declared, were violated by the several acts which Parliament had passed. Only by the repeal of these could harmony between Great Britain and the colonies be restored. If England should attempt to execute the laws against Massachusetts by force, the Continental Congress declared, "In such a case all America ought to support Massachusetts in their opposition."

This was, in effect, an act of war. Before Congress adjourned it provided for a meeting of another Congress, on

May 10, 1775, to receive the King's answer to the petition.

Neither in England or America were the people wholly united. Parliament had a large majority favoring the radical measures of King George III, but some of the greatest statesmen, like Pitt, Burke, and Fox, showed favor to the colonies. In America, the people were divided. The majority who opposed the acts of England were called "patriots." A large number who sided with the King and Parliament were called "loyalists," or "Tories."

In Massachusetts, Governor Gage found it difficult to enforce the laws and punish the rebellious colonists. Many of the King's judges, sheriffs and custom-house officers were forced, by mobs, to resign and close their offices, temporarily suspending the operation of the government. Tories were driven from their estates and took refuge with the British army.

After calling the Massachusetts legislature to assemble at Salem in October 1774, Gage postponed it due to the angry tone of the people. The legislature met without the governor's consent and organized a new government, with John Hancock at its head. A committee of safety was appointed to prepare for possible war.

The patriots began to select officers and collect arms to drill the militia. Massachusetts called for an army of 12,000 troops, called "minutemen," ready at a moment's notice to march to any point of danger.

*INDEPENDENCE HALL IN PHILADELPHIA*

*THE CONTINENTAL CONGRESS IN SESSION*

# LEXINGTON, CONCORD AND THE SECOND CONGRESS

By April 1775, the patriots had collected a quantity of guns and military supplies at Concord, some 20 miles from Boston. General Gage was directed to seize the stores and arrest John Hancock and Samuel Adams. London papers boasted that the heads of these two prominent "rebels" would soon be seen in the city. Gage sent a force of 800 men to destroy the supplies at Concord, and on the way to arrest Hancock and Adams, who were at Lexington.

The British troops left Boston secretly about midnight, April 18, 1775, but the patriots were on the watch. A sentinel in the tower of the Old North Church in Boston flashed the news with signal lanterns to watchful couriers in Charlestown, that the British had started to move. The messengers, among them Paul Revere (whose name has been preserved by Longfellow's poem about the events of that night, called "Paul Revere's Ride"), galloped through country and town, spreading the alarm. Revere and William Dawes, another messenger, were captured a few miles beyond Lexington and taken back to

*DANIEL FRENCH'S MINUTEMAN STATUE*

Boston as prisoners. Dr. Samuel Prescott carried the news of the attack to Concord.

The British arrived at Lexington at dawn on April 19, where a number of minutemen confronted them. "Disperse, you rebels!" was the shrill cry of Major Pitcairn, the British officer, but the patriots did not obey. The British fired into the crowd, killing eight and wounding ten. The patriots retreated and Adams and Hancock escaped. The British went on to Concord, destroyed the supplies, set fire to the courthouse, and started back to Boston. However, their withdrawal would not be as easy as the morning's fight. Minutemen flocked to the scene and opened fire on the retreating foe. The British march to Lexington and Concord was a holiday jaunt. That from Lexington was a flight for life.

From farmhouse and hedge, from bush and rock, tree and fence, the colonists poured deadly musket fire into the English column. Lord Percy counterattacked at Lexington with a thousand reinforcements from Boston, but he could not break the fighting spirit of the patriots They bore down on every side and drove the British to Boston, with a loss of nearly 300 dead and wounded. All night long the Minutemen continued to pour in from throughout Massachusetts. The next morning found the "redcoats" bottled up in Boston by the Yankee patriots. (The British soldiers were called "redcoats" because they wore red uniforms.)

News of these events aroused the entire country. The British had given the challenge of war, and the patriots hastened to accept it.

The Revolutionary War had begun at Lexington and Concord, and it soon spread. On May 10, 1775, Ethan Allen (1738-1789) and his Vermont volunteers known as the "Green Mountain Boys," accompanied by Benedict Arnold (1741-1801), surprised the British garrison at Fort Ticonderoga.

They managed to get into the fort unobserved and captured it without the loss of a single man. General Delaplace,

*THE LEGENDARY "MIDNIGHT RIDE" OF PAUL REVERE TOOK PLACE ON APRIL 18, 1775*

the commander, was still in bed. A knock at the door and a summons to surrender were his first warnings. Amazed and dazed, with trousers in hand, he said to Allen, "Surrender to whom and by whose authority?"

"To me," Ethan Allen is said to have replied, "in the name of the Great Jehovah and the Continental Congress!"

It is important to point out that at the time, the area that is now Vermont (which literally means "green mountains") was part of New Hampshire.

Crown Point was captured a few days later by a band of patriots under Seth Warner.

The Second Continental Congress met as planned on May 10, 1775, the same day that Ticonderoga surrendered. The Congress had planned to meet to hear the answer from the King on the petitions of the First Continental Con-

*THE MINUTEMEN FACED BRITISH REGULARS AT LEXINGTON ON APRIL 19, 1775.*

gress. George III's answer came in the form of more troops to subdue the colonists.

The First Continental Congress debated, petitioned, and issued a Declaration of Rights. The Second Continental Congress was a Congress of action. It became the general ruling body of the colonies. It set to work with an energy seldom equalled by any legislative body, to make the war and to direct the general affairs of the colonies.

Except for short intermissions, it would remain in session at various places until near the close of the war in 1781. The principal tasks undertaken by the Congress in the early 1775 session at Philadelphia were to select George Washington as commander-in-chief of the army, and to issue currency in the form of bills of credit. Washington served without pay. His salary was fixed at $500 a month, but in accepting the command, Washington said he did not wish to make any profit out of the position, but would ask Congress to pay only his expenses.

The Second Continental Congress created a post office department with Benjamin Franklin at the head. Still professing loyalty to the mother country, it sent a last petition to the King and issued addresses to the people of Great Britain, Ireland, and Canada.

*ETHAN ALLEN DEMANDED THE MIDNIGHT SURRENDER OF TICONDEROGA ON MAY 10, 1775.*

# THE BATTLE AND AFTERMATH OF BUNKER HILL

The second battle of the American Revolution was fought on June 17, 1775, before Washington took command of the army. Minutemen, learning of the British plans, sent a force of 1,500 troops under Colonel Prescott, on the night of June 16, to take possession of Bunker Hill, a strategic location immediately north of Boston. By mistake or design, Prescott passed Bunker Hill and began to fortify Breed's Hill, nearer to Boston. All night long the Americans worked, building breastworks. The British were stunned to find these fortifications in place the next morning.

The British bombarded the hill from Boston and from warships in Boston Harbor. In the afternoon, 3,000 veteran British troops under General Sir William Howe (1729-1814), crossed from Boston to drive the Americans out. Howe advanced swiftly and confidently, expecting the Americans to run. Prescott's orders were, "Don't fire till you see the whites of their eyes."

When the enemy was within 50 yards of the Patriots, a terrific volley of fire from the American muskets quickly thinned their ranks. The British retreated, reformed, and advanced, but once again they were driven back with heavy losses. A third attempt ended in success, as the Continentals ran out of powder and were without bayonets. For a time they defended themselves with the butts of their guns, but finally they withdrew. The British losses were over 1,000, while American losses were fewer than half that number.

Though a military loss, the Battle of Bunker Hill was a moral victory for the Americans. The bravery of the patriots

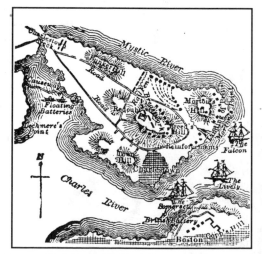

**THE BUNKER HILL BATTLEFIELD**

forever silenced the slurs so freely used by the British about the valor of Americans. It dispelled all doubt about the ability of the Minutemen to meet the British regulars, and built up the hope and confidence of the Americans.

Washington reached Cambridge, and under the shade of a great elm took command of the army on July 3. The soldiers were poorly armed and without discipline, but Lexington and Bunker Hill demonstrated their will to fight. The need for ammunition was a serious drawback; factories for arms and gunpowder were set up in the colonies, and were gradually supplied. Foundries in New York began to produce a number of cannons; General Henry Knox (1750-1806) brought 40 heavy guns to Boston on sleds through the forests from Ticonderoga.

The patriots purchased powder from Ireland and the Bahamas; a considerable quantity was seized from British vessels before their crews knew that American privateers were on the seas.

*AFTER MANY FRUITLESS CHARGES UP THE DIFFICULT SLOPES OF BUNKER HILL, THE BRITISH WERE FINALLY ABLE TO OVER-WHELM THE HARD-FIGHTING MINUTEMEN.*

At the same time, Congress feared that the British in Canada, under Sir Guy Carleton, would invade New York before Washington could bring the army up to strength.

To prevent this, two expeditions were sent into Canada to capture Montreal and Quebec. The first, under the command of Richard Montgomery (1738-1775), set out from Ticonderoga; he defeated Carleton near the St. Lawrence River. He captured Montreal in November, and in December laid siege to Quebec.

The second force, under Benedict Arnold, went by boat from Newburyport to Maine. They worked their way up the Kennebec River and through dense forests. After six weeks, the weary, ragged force linked up with Montgomery near Quebec. They assaulted the city, but the attack ended in failure; Montgomery was killed and Arnold wounded. In the spring, the American troops would be forced to retreat from Canada.

Meanwhile, the British were not without their own difficulties. One of the major troubles for General Howe, who had succeeded General Gage, was the difficulty of getting food for his army.

Washington spent the winter of 1775-1776 drilling, disciplining and equipping the troops for battle.

*AMERICAN ARTILLERY OPENS FIRE ON THE BRITISH IN QUEBEC*

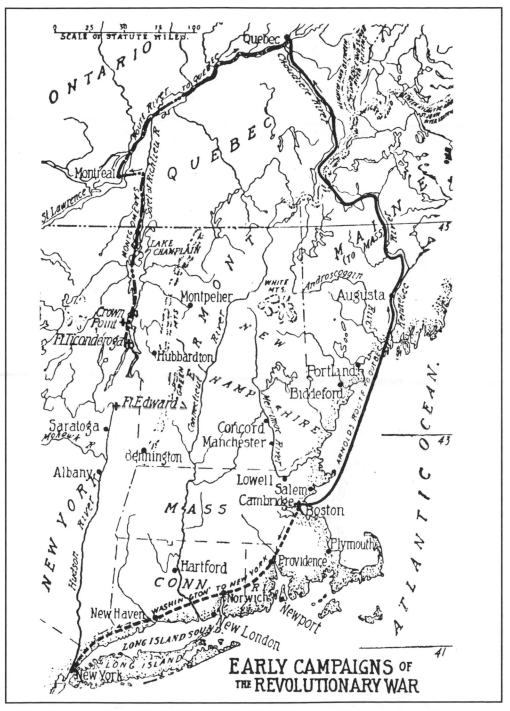

EARLY CAMPAIGNS OF THE REVOLUTIONARY WAR

*THE ROUTE OF ARNOLD AND MONTGOMERY TO QUEBEC, AND WASHINGTON TO NEW YORK*

# THE DECLARATION OF INDEPENDENCE

By the end of 1775, it was clear that the British would not give in to the colonial demands for freedom and autonomy in their own affairs. King George would settle for nothing less than total subjugation; and he would settle things with an iron fist. For the Americans, 1776 would be a year of decision. They would declare that they were no longer Englishmen or subjects of England's monarch. The shots fired in 1775 from Boston to Quebec were only the beginning.

The beginning of the year found the British firmly in control of major cities such as Boston. On the night of March 4, 1776, while a cannon barrage held the attention of the British, the Americans secretly occupied Dorchester Heights south of Boston. Working quickly, they placed a line of cannons overlooking the city and harbor. Boston then lay at the mercy of Washington's troops. Howe had been "outgeneraled."

An attempt to take the hill would end in disaster, so Howe angrily concluded that he'd have to abandon the city. On March 17, he evacuated his army by sea to Halifax, carrying with him 1,500 Tories. Washington took possession of Boston, but a few days later he marched to New York City, which, he believed, would be attacked next by the British.

By July 1776, the unrelenting attitude of King George III had produced a great change of sentiment in America. As late as the middle of 1775, the

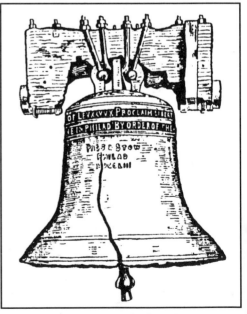

**THE LIBERTY BELL**

*JOHN HANCOCK'S SIGNATURE WAS PROMINENT AMONG THOSE OF THE SIGNERS.*

29

colonists would have been satisfied with a redress of grievances, but things started to change as they began to fight for their rights as Englishmen.

When the King called them "rebels" and sent troops to put down the "rebellion," sentiment grew rapidly for independence. A pamphlet called "Common Sense," written by Thomas Paine (1737-1809), strongly advocated separation from England It was read by tens of thousands, and expressed what most of the colonists really felt.

Virginia instructed her delegates in Congress to vote for independence. On June 7, Richard Henry Lee proposed the resolution that read:

"Resolved, That these, United Colonies are, and of right ought to be, free and independent states; that they be absolved from all allegiance to the British and that all political connection between them and the state of Great Britain is, and ought to be, totally dissolved."

John Adams of Massachusetts seconded the resolution. On July 2, a vote was taken, and Lee's resolution of independence was adopted. Meanwhile, a committee of five was appointed to draft what would be a formal Declaration of Independence.

The members of the committee were Thomas Jefferson, John Adams, Roger Sherman, Benjamin Franklin and Robert Livingston. Thomas Jefferson (1743-1726), as the chairman, undertook the task of writing the Declaration. A Virginia lawyer and legislator, Jefferson is well remembered for his role in the American Revolution and as the third president of the United States. He was also an accomplished scientist and philosopher, as well as being a professional architect and city planner. Of him

*THOMAS JEFFERSON DRAFTED THE DECLARATION.*

it was said: "He could calculate an eclipse, survey an estate, tie an artery, plan an edifice, try a cause, break a horse, dance a minuet, and play a violin."

Jefferson was a master in the use of English, and was fluent in several other languages. As Washington is sometimes called the sword, so Jefferson may be called the pen of the Revolution. With only a few minor changes, the Declaration of Independence, as drafted by him, was adopted by the Continental Congress on July 4, 1776.

John Hancock of Massachusetts, President of the Congress, signed the Declaration first; and his signature appears the largest (see the facsimile on page 29).

He explained that he did this so that the "King of England could read it without his spectacles."

The bell in the Old State House in Philadelphia — now known as "the Liberty Bell" — rang out the joyous tidings to the people. It sounded the message which had been cast on its side 24 years before: "Proclaim liberty throughout the land, unto all the inhabitants thereof." The bell was rung so loud that it cracked.

Some weeks later, on August 2, when all the members of Congress signed the printed copies of the Declaration, Hancock remarked, "We must all hang together."

"Yes," said Franklin, "we had better hang together or we shall all *HANG* separately."

Through the Declaration of Independence, the United Colonies became the United States of America. However, it would take five more years of war to convince King George III and his Parliament of this fact.

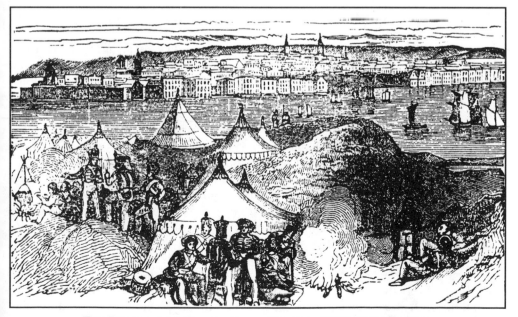

*THE BRITISH CAMPED ACROSS THE CHARLES RIVER FROM BOSTON.*

# WASHINGTON'S FIRST CAMPAIGNS

After reaching New York in June 1776, Washington built Fort Lee and Fort Washington (named for his father, not himself) north of the city on opposite banks of the Hudson River. He also fortified Brooklyn Heights in the western part of Long Island. He had correctly judged the British plans, for the fleet carrying Howe's army arrived on Staten Island on July 2. It was joined by another fleet and a force from England under Howe's brother, Admiral Richard Howe (1726-1799).

These troops were, in turn, augmented by forces supplied by the German grand duchy of Hesse. The combined strength of General and Admiral Howe's British forces, including the Hessians, stood at 30,000. To oppose them Washington had only about 17,000; approximately one third of them were on Long Island, New York under the command of General Israel Putnam.

The object of the British invasion force was to seize New York and the areas adjacent to the Hudson, to open up a line of communication with Canada. This would separate New England, the hotbed of the rebellion, from the rest of the colonies. It was imaged that this could be accomplished quite easily and quickly because there was a large concentration of Tories and Tory sympathizers in New York City.

Meanwhile, the Hudson, Lake Champlain, and the St. Lawrence would provide the British with an excellent natural defensive line and also a good route over which to carry troops and supplies to and from Canada. With New York subdued, they then hoped to attack Massachusetts and crush out the rebellion.

Having landed an army more than twice as large as the American force on Long Island, Howe totally defeated Putnam's troops on August 27 and drove them behind their barricades.

The Americans were hemmed in on every side and a mile of open water separated them from the rest of Washington's troops. A superior land army opposed them on one side, while a large fleet opposed the other. It seemed that the whole force would be compelled to surrender in a short time. However, Washington devised a scheme to save the army. Leaving the campfires still burning, under cover of a dense fog and a dark night, Washington crossed to New

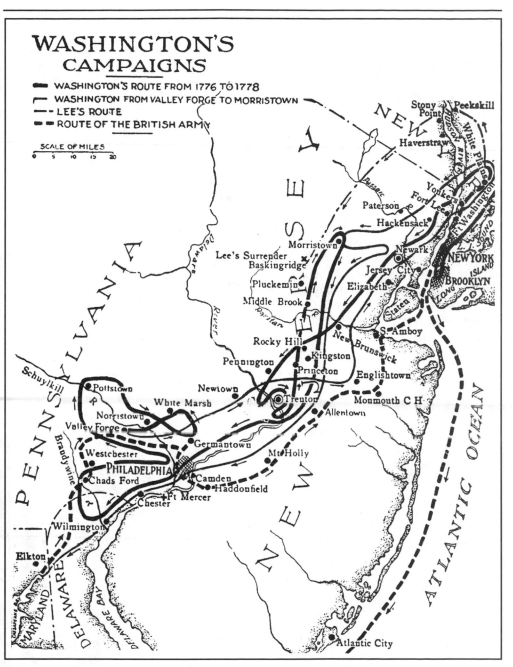

# WASHINGTON'S CAMPAIGNS

- ▰▰ WASHINGTON'S ROUTE FROM 1776 TO 1778
- ⌐ WASHINGTON FROM VALLEY FORGE TO MORRISTOWN
- –·– LEE'S ROUTE
- ▬ ▬ ROUTE OF THE BRITISH ARMY

SCALE OF MILES
0   5   10   15   20

*WASHINGTON'S 1776-1778 CAMPAIGN INVOLVED A MARCH FROM BROOKLYN TO WHITE PLAINS, ACROSS NEW JERSEY INTO PENNSYLVANIA, AND THEN TO TRENTON AND BACK TO PENNSYLVANIA. AFTER THE BATTLE OF PRINCETON, IT WAS BACK TO PHILADELPHIA, BRANDYWINE, AND VALLEY FORGE. AFTER THE DIFFICULT WINTER AT VALLEY FORGE, THE ARMY MARCHED ACROSS NEW JERSEY TO MONMOUTH, WHITE PLAINS, AND BACK TO MORRISTOWN.*

33

York and then escaped north along the Hudson. The next morning, when Howe moved to capture the "nest of rebels," they were gone.

The British then took possession of Long Island and New York City, but they had failed to capture the American troops. American forces were still in possession of the key points along the Hudson, such as Fort Lee, Fort Washington, West Point, and North Castle. After Washington left New York, some irresponsible parties set fire to the city, and a large part was burned. When Howe issued a proclamation promising pardon to all who would lay down their arms, the colonists refused any pardon at the sacrifice of their rights.

During the New York campaign, Washington needed information concerning the movements of the British; a young patriot soldier, named Nathan Hale (1755-1776), volunteered for a reconnaissance mission. On his return trip to American lines, he was captured by the British. Tried and convicted as a spy, he was sentenced to be hanged. As he was going to his death he said, "I regret that I have but one life to give to my country."

Even as Washington's mobile forces moved freely on the east side of the Hudson River, Howe sent a British strike force under General Charles Cornwallis (1738-1805) to rout him. Washington withdrew from Fort Lee, and Cornwallis, having learned the layout of Fort Washington's defenses from a deserter. He succeeded in taking the fort on November 12, 1776.

The loss of these forts, along with 3,000 prisoners taken at Fort Washing-

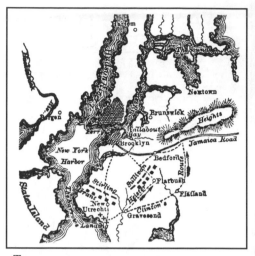

*THE RELATIVE POSITIONS OF THE OPPOSING FORCES AT THE TIME OF THE BATTLE OF LONG ISLAND*

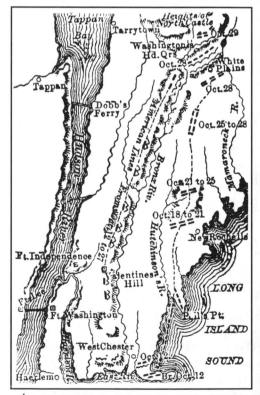

*AN OVERVIEW OF THE RELATIVE POSITIONS AROUND NEW YORK CITY, 1776-1777*

**GENERAL GEORGE WASHINGTON, THE CONTINENTAL ARMY COMMANDER-IN-CHIEF**

ton, was a terrible blow. A part of Washington's army was overtaken and defeated at White Plains and he found himself in retreat.

Washington moved his troops toward Philadelphia, at that time the capital of the colonies.

The retreat of Washington's army across New Jersey has had few parallels in history. It was a game of "hide-and-seek" between a ragged, hungry, unpaid and poorly armed band of patriots on the one hand and a large army of well-drilled and finely equipped European troops on the other.

Washington could not afford to get caught in a fire-fight with five times his own number, so he acted on the principle that "He who fights and runs away may live to fight another day."

More than once the forward echelons of Cornwallis's army overtook the rear of Washington's army as his troops lingered to burn bridges or obstruct the British march. Washington sent word to General Charles Lee, who was at North Castle with 7,000 troops, asking him to link up his forces with Washington's. Lee disobeyed, apparently hoping that by withholding his own forces, Washington would be defeated and Lee could succeed him as commander-in-chief. Lee finally crossed the Hudson on December 2, 1776 and moved leisurely across to New Jersey.

While stopping overnight at a small inn at Basking Ridge, he was captured by a party of British dragoons. General John Sullivan (1740-1795), who was Lee's second in command, escaped with

*GENERAL WASHINGTON LEADING HIS TROOPS IN THE BATTLE OF PRINCETON.*

3,000 troops and hurried to join Washington, who had reached the Delaware River in safety.

By this time, the patriotic cause seemed lost and the British generals were even preparing to return some of their forces to England. It was a Christmas season of gloom and distress, but soon it was to be changed into a season of rejoicing using Washington's military skill. On reaching the Delaware at Trenton, Washington seized every boat he could find up and down the river, and crossed into Pennsylvania, cutting off the British pursuit. Unable to pursue Washington across the river, Cornwallis distributed his troops in several towns in New Jersey and waited at Trenton for the river to freeze so he could again take up the chase. On December 26, 1776, reinforced by Lee's troops, Washington planned a surprise for the British before they would recover from their Christmas festivities. On Christmas night, amid drifting ice, he crossed the Delaware with 2,400 hand-picked troops and marched nine miles in a blinding snowstorm. They surprised and captured a force of 1,000 Hessians with only two killed and two wounded. Cornwallis hurried a large force to the scene, but Washington, his troops, and the prisoners were safe across the river.

A few days later, Washington again crossed the Delaware into New Jersey. With his strong force, Cornwallis was confident of victory and anxious to do battle. Only a small creek divided the two armies on the night of January 2, 1777 when Cornwallis wrote "At last, we have run down the old fox and we will bag him in the morning."

However, Washington was up to his old tricks. Leaving his campfires burning, Washington made a forced march to Princeton, and there attacked and defeated the troops Cornwallis had left to guard his line of defense. The sound of the American cannons at Princeton was the first that Cornwallis knew of the fact that Washington had slipped away.

After the battle of Princeton Washington went into winter quarters among the hills around Morristown, while the British retired to New Brunswick and Amboy. These brilliant victories produced a wonderful effect. Joy, hope, and confidence were restored, money was raised and more troops enlisted.

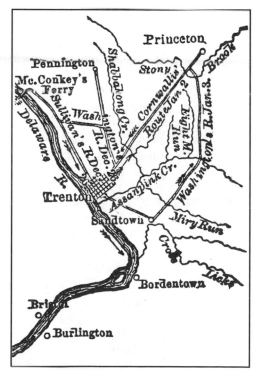

AN OVERVIEW OF THE NEW JERSEY BATTLE-FRONT AROUND PRINCETON AND TRENTON

# THE WAR'S NORTHERN FRONT

During the summer of 1777 the British began a second attempt to cut New England off from the rest of the colonies. The main army, under General John Burgoyne (1722-1792), who had succeeded Carleton, was to invade New York State from Canada by way of Lake Champlain and the Hudson. A second army, under General Barry St. Leger (1737-1789), was to sail up the St. Lawrence, through Lake Ontario to Oswego, across the state and down the Mohawk Valley, stirring up the powerful Indian tribes on the way. A third prong was to sail up the Hudson River from New York City. All were to unite at Albany. The plan was simple and sufficiently complete, if carried out, to bring the state of New York into line for the British.

With an army of 8,000 men, General Burgoyne left Canada. The American army, under General Arthur St. Clair (1736-1818), hastily fled southward, abandoning Fort Ticonderoga and 93 cannons. At Skeenesboro, the British fleet captured a large stock of supplies and provisions which had been taken from Ticonderoga by boat.

The rear of the retreating army was overtaken at Hubbardston, and severely mauled, but it finally reached Fort Edward, where General Philip Schuyler (1733-1804) was in command.

The entire American army did not exceed 4,000 men. The cause seemed dark indeed to the colonists as they thought of the British, with their Native American allies, overrunning the state.

*THE MARQUIS OF LAFAYETTE*

*THE SURRENDER OF BRITAIN'S GENERAL BURGOYNE ON OCTOBER 17, 1777*

The first feeling of panic soon gave way to indignation and determined resistance as the militia of New York and New England joined Schuyler's army.

The progress of the British was hindered as Schuyler's people destroyed bridges, felled trees across roads, obstructed fords, cut off the food supply, and made life a burden to the invader.

Burgoyne learned that the Americans had collected a supply of food at Bennington, a small town in what is now southwestern Vermont, but which was then part of New Hampshire. He sent Colonel Baum with 1,000 Hessians to capture these supplies. Colonel John Stark (1728-1822), the head of the state militia, the Green Mountain Boys,

defeated and captured nearly the entire force on August 15. This brilliant victory reduced the British army in numbers, and greatly encouraged the patriots.

It was also in 1777 that Ethan Allen declared Vermont to be independent, not only from England but from New Hampshire. Allen's "Republic of New Connecticut" entered the Union in 1791 as Vermont, the fourteenth state.

Meanwhile, St. Leger advanced from Oswego and laid siege to Fort Stanwix. General Nicholas Herkimer (1728-1777) gathered a state militia force and marched to the aid of the fort. He was ambushed on August 6 and defeated, but he took the pressure off the troops defending the fort, and they beat back

*SOUNDING THE ALARM AT FORT SCHUYLER*

the British attackers. It was at this battle that the American flag — with the ring of thirteen stars on a blue field and thirteen red and white stripes — first flew.

General Schuyler then sent Benedict Arnold and three regiments up the Mohawk Valley to relieve Fort Stanwix. Arnold sent a messenger ahead to announce that a very large American army was at hand. The British and Native Americans, became alarmed and fled, leaving supplies behind. Arnold returned to the Hudson in time to take part in the battle of Saratoga.

As the cold winds of autumn began to blow, Burgoyne saw the dangers grow thick and fast about him. Baum's army had been destroyed and St. Leger's defeated. The Native American allies began to desert. Food had become scarce. Reinforcements flocked to the Americans until they outnumbered the British. Benjamin Lincoln (1733-1810) came with 2,000 New England troops. Daniel Morgan (1736-1702) of Virginia brought a rifle corps of 500 sharpshooters, while Arnold's regiments were on the way back from the victory at Fort Stanwix.

General Howe, who was to come up the Hudson, moved against Philadelphia instead. He sent General Henry Clinton (1738-1795) up the river, but he was too late to reach Burgoyne. Advance and retreat were equally perilous.

Burgoyne made two desperate attempts to drive back the Americans; one at Bemis Heights on September 19 and at Stillwater on October 7, but each was defeated. He withdrew to Saratoga, where he finally surrendered on October 17, 1777. Accepting his sword was General Horatio Gates (1727-1706), who had succeeded General Schuyler, but credit for the victory was due largely to Morgan, Arnold, and Schuyler.

At the beginning of the campaign, Burgoyne boasted that he would eat Christmas dinner in Albany. He did in fact eat his dinner there, but as a prisoner of war.

Meanwhile, on the Pennsylvania front, the fortunes of the Americans were not shining so brightly. British efforts to take Philadelphia by marching across New Jersey had failed because Washington blocked the way, but Howe would form a new plan. Leaving Clinton in command at New York to help Burgoyne, he took 16,000 troops by sea, ascended the Chesapeake Bay to Elkton, and then set out on foot for Philadelphia. The route by the Delaware River and Bay would have been more direct, but the river was guarded by strong forts, so General Howe chose to go by way of the Chesapeake.

As the fleet moved southward, signal-fires along the Jersey shore told of its progress. The news was carried inland by messengers. When Washington learned of Howe's movements, he started on a rapid march for Philadelphia. Passing through Philadelphia, Chester and Wilmington, he drove in to make a stand at Chad's Fort on Brandywine Creek.

In the Battle of Brandywine on September 11, 1777, Washington was defeated. He retreated first to Philadelphia, and later to Pottstown. Congress was evacuated from Philadelphia and fled first to Lancaster, then to York, Pennsylvania.

The British entered Philadelphia on September 26. On October 4, 1777, while some of the British were making an attack on Forts Mifflin and Mercer, which guarded the Delaware River, Washington attacked the British army at Germantown (now part of Philadelphia), but was forced to withdraw. Washington, though defeated, was able to continue harassing the British. This compelled Howe to request more troops from New York.

These troops, diverted from Burgoyne, sealed his fate when they were sent to Howe. Burgoyne was forced to wait until fresh troops could be brought from England; they arrived too late to save him.

Despite the setback at Philadelphia, the series of British defeats that climaxed at Saratoga had cost the British 10,000 men as casualties or prisoners, and had broken their offensive in the north. King George III was stunned. He came forward with a proposal for peace, promising not to tax the colonies, to give them representation in Parliament, and to grant pardon to all. Ironically, he was ready to grant everything that had been asked by the First Continental Congress — and more. Everything, that is, except independence. It was too late.

Saratoga is regarded as one of the most decisive battles of the war. It brought hope and confidence to the colonists, doubt and despair to the British, and ultimately resulted in an alliance between America and France. The French had no fondness for the British before, but Saratoga finally convinced them of American competence and American resolve.

Soon after the Declaration of Independence was proclaimed, Benjamin Franklin was sent as a commissioner to get aid from France. All he could secure was secret help in the form of war materiel and loans.

The surrender of Burgoyne made success seem possible, even certain, for America, if France would give her aid. France's King Louis XVI (1754-1793) openly announced support for the American cause and signed a treaty of alliance on February 6, 1778. He recognized the independence of the colonies, increased his loans to them, and prepared to send a fleet and an army to America. This, of course, meant that a state of war now existed between France and England. Before peace was restored, Spain and Holland were also at war with England.

However, even before the formal French alliance, a number of Frenchmen had come over to help the Americans. Among them were the great military strategist the Marquis de Lafayette (1757-1734). Another important leader, Baron Johann DeKalb (1720-1780), the Bavarian-born French general who gave valiant service in the southern campaign, also came to America's aid.

Other European military officers who fought with the Americans included Baron Friedreich Wilhelm von Steuben (1730-1794), a Prussian officer who joined Washington's army at Valley Forge, and proved of great value as a drill-master. Two Polish officers, engineer Thaddeus Kosciusko (1746-1817) and Count Casimir Pulaski (1748-1779). Pulaski served at the battles of Brandywine and Charleston; and at Savannah, where he lost his life.

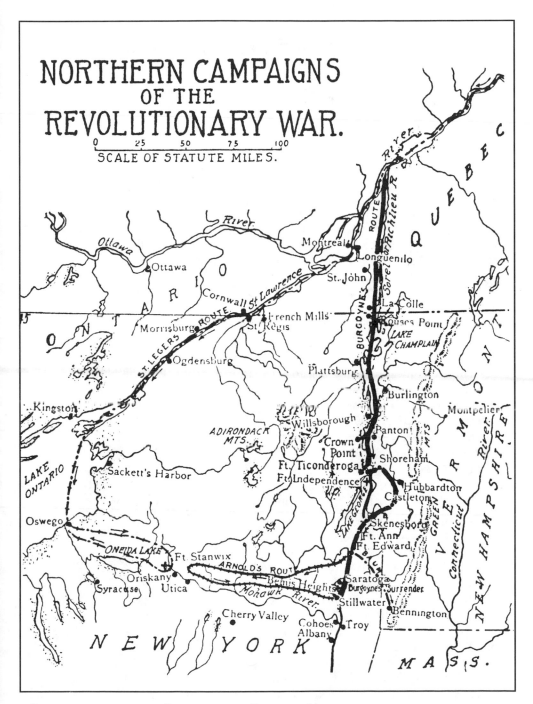

*CROWNED BY VICTORY AT SARATOGA, THE COLONISTS' NORTHERN CAMPAIGN WAS A SUCCESS.*

# THE CAMPAIGNS
## OF 1778

Defeated in a series of battles, but with his army still largely intact, Washington went into 1777-1778 winter quarters at Valley Forge, about 20 miles northwest of Philadelphia. It was to be a cold winter of bitterness and suffering. The troops were in rags. Their marches could be traced by trails of blood left on the snow from sore and shoeless feet. In a letter to Congress, Washington said that 2,998 troops were unfit for duty because they were barefoot. Often the soldiers went hungry. At one time there was no bread for three days. In three weeks of piercing cold, without fighting, they lost 2,000 troops from hardships and exposure.

Amid all these sufferings, this band of patriots, defeated but still unbroken in spirit, hung together. Never did braver or truer troops under a greater leader bear arms for a better cause.

The British, at the same time, were living in comfort, ease and plenty, in and around Philadelphia.

In the midst of these misfortunes some of the officers formed a plot to replace Washington with Gates. Wash-ington was still very popular with the troops, and when the plot was exposed there was such a wave of indignation among the people that it failed.

When the British learned of the French alliance and that a French fleet and army were on their way to enter Delaware Bay to cooperate with Washington, they decided on a tactical withdrawal from Philadelphia. Sir Henry Clinton, who had succeeded Howe, set out on a forced march for New York.

**GEORGE ROGERS CLARK**

Washington followed. Moving rapidly, he overtook the British at Monmouth, New Jersey on June 28, 1778.

Washington would probably have achieved a victory had it not been for the treachery of an American General, Charles Lee. General Lee had been a prisoner of the British from December 1776 to April 1778, and was ransomed for General Prescott, a British officer. At the moment when a flank of the British army could have been cut off, Lee disobeyed Washington's orders, and, when the British opened fire, ordered a retreat. However, when Washington arrived, his soldiers put the British on the run, but Clinton's force remained intact. For his conduct at the battle of Monmouth, Lee was sent to the rear, court-martialed, and later dismissed from service.

While in Philadelphia, the British officers were wined and dined by Tories and Americans in sympathy with the crown. The day of reckoning came when Clinton withdrew from the city. No less than 3,000 loyalists, fearing to remain, went with him. Of those who remained, a few were hanged and others banished.

The main body of the British armies in the north were now consolidated in

*THE AMERICAN CAVALRY CHARGE AT MONMOUTH, NEW JERSEY ON JUNE 28, 1778*

New York City. Washington stretched his lines from Morristown, New Jersey to White Plains, New York. For the next two years, these respective forces were to remain in position without a major battle.

The French fleet pursued the British to New York, but their largest ships could not pass over the bar to enter the harbor. An alternate action was planned to drive the British from Newport, Rhode Island, by the combined efforts of the fleet and a land force under General John Sullivan.

The English fleet was sent to protect Newport, but before a battle occurred, a storm dispersed the rival fleets, greatly injuring some of the French ships. Admiral Charles d'Estaing (1729-1794), the French commander, took his fleet to Boston for repairs. He later went to the West Indies to protect French interests there, so Sullivan's fleet was compelled to retreat.

Meanwhile, the Tories and Native Americans of central and western New York began burning property and killing Americans. In the summer of 1778 a large force, led by John Butler, marched into the beautiful Wyoming Valley in northeastern Pennsylvania and committed several massacres. During the same year, Cherry Valley, New York, suffered a similar fate at the hands of Tories and Native Americans led by Mohawk chief Thayendanegea (1742-1807), who had been educated in England and went by the name Joseph Brant.

In 1779, Washington sent General Sullivan with an army of 5,000 to put an end to these bloody raids. Near the present site of Elmira, New York, he administered a crushing defeat to the allied bands of Native Americans and Tories.

In the remote areas west of the Appalachian Mountain Range, pioneers were working for the American cause. Among these was Daniel Boone (1734-

*DANIEL BOONE WAS CAPTURED BY THE CHEROKEES, BUT MANAGED TO ESCAPE.*

1820), the noted frontiersman, who had moved into this region with other pioneers in 1775. In 1776, when the legislature of Virginia created the county of Kentucky, these pioneers waged successful war against the Native American allies of the British. John Sevier and James Robertson were prominent in defeating the Cherokee Native Americans in the territory which later became Tennessee.

George Rogers Clark (1752-1818), was another Virginian who had settled in Kentucky. Acting under the authority of Patrick Henry, then the governor of Virginia, he performed great service to the new nation by winning the country north of the Ohio River for the United States.

Clark secretly raised an army of volunteers and attacked the British in what is now the state of Ohio. He travelled downstream from Pittsburgh to the mouth of the Cumberland and marched cross-country, taking the towns and forts held by the British and making a friendly call on the Spaniards at St. Louis.

He then marched to Vincennes, where he met and defeated General Hamilton, the British commandant, who had come from Detroit with 500 men to aid in the defense of Vincennes. Through Clark's efforts, British power was completely broken south of the Great Lakes. These victories also served to strengthen American claims to the territory as far west as the Mississippi.

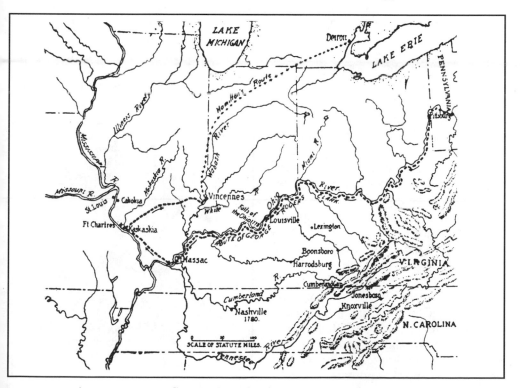

*AN OVERVIEW OF GEORGE ROGERS CLARK'S CAMPAIGN IN THE WEST*

# ACTIONS IN THE NORTH DURING 1779

To reinforce his positions on the Hudson, Washington had built two forts above West Point; one at Stony Point and the other at Verplanck's Point. However, the British seized Stony Point before it was completed and Washington sent General "Mad Anthony" Wayne (1745-1796) to recapture it. At midnight on July 15, 1779, 1,200 hand-picked commandos, carrying empty guns, climbed the steep sides of the precipice, and used fixed bayonets in a brilliant charge that recaptured the fort and took 500 prisoners.

Another daring exploit was achieved by Henry Lee (1756-1818). Lee earned the popular nickname "Light Horse Harry" after he stormed and captured Paulus Hook, a stronghold on the New Jersey side of the Hudson opposite New York City, from which the British had been raiding New Jersey farms.

Also during 1779, British commander-in-chief General Clinton had sent a marauding expedition to plunder and ravage the farms and towns of Connecticut. He hoped to draw Washington from his positions north and west of New York City, but news of the British disaster at Stony Point put an end to this action.

In the midst of these conflicts, Benedict Arnold committed the despicable act of treason that has made his name virtually synonymous with the world "traitor" in the American dictionary. Arnold had proven himself to be one of the bravest and ablest of the American generals. He had distinguished himself at Quebec and Saratoga and gave promise of still greater service to the nation when

*JOHN PAUL JONES*

Washington placed him in command at Philadelphia in 1778, after the British withdrew to New York.

Here, Arnold had married the daughter of a prominent Tory and lived beyond his means. He turned to corruption to raise money, was caught, tried by a court-martial and sentenced to be reprimanded. Washington was lenient with punishment and gave Arnold a second chance. Washington, who had every confidence in him, placed Arnold in command at West Point in 1780. He did not yet realize that Arnold had begun the process of selling out to the British.

Arnold secretly offered to surrender West Point. Major John Andre (1751-1780), Adjutant-General of the British army, met Arnold near Stony Point to arrange the terms of surrender, but on his way back, he was arrested by three Americans who were watching for British cattle thieves. In his socks, they found papers in Arnold's handwriting. Arnold heard news of the arrest, and he fled his post, escaping to join the British army. The British paid him a large sum of money, and he served as an officer in their army to the end of the war, fighting his own countrymen. At the end of the

*JOHN PAUL JONES AND HIS MEN BOARD THE* **Serapis** *FROM THE* **Bon Homme Richard.** *JONES CAPTURED THE* **Serapis,** *ALTHOUGH HIS OWN VESSEL SANK.*

war, he took refuge in England, where he would live out his days in sorrow and remorse. Andre was hung as a spy.

Meanwhile, the United States had recognized the need to develop sea power to counter the powerful British Royal Navy, which controlled both the Atlantic sea lanes and the American shoreline. Late in 1775, Congress had ordered thirteen warships to be built. Before these were finished, however, several merchant vessels were fitted up and sailed from Philadelphia to prey on British commerce in the West Indies. Each of the seacoast states fitted out one or more warships.

After the Declaration of Independence, Congress had issued "letters of marque and reprisal," which gave the right to private persons to fit out ships to seize the enemy's vessels, and share with the government the fruits of such victories. In this way, a great deal of damage was done to British commerce. However, the American navy could in no way cope with the formidable British fleets, but could only prey on unguarded merchantmen or detached cruisers. Nearly all of the American vessels were captured or destroyed before the close of the war, but the French fleets became a powerful factor in wielding independence.

The most brilliant of all victories on the sea was achieved by Admiral John Paul Jones (1747-1792). In command of the *Ranger* in 1775, he made one of the most remarkable cruises in naval history; darting in and out of the coast of the British Isles, setting fire to shipping, destroying four British vessels, capturing an armed cruiser, and returning in safety to France.

In 1779, through the aid of Benjamin Franklin, who was the American ambassador to France, Jones obtained a fleet of five warships in France and set out to prey on British vessels. His flagship was named *Bon Homme Richard* (the good man Richard), in honor of Franklin's "Poor Richard's Almanac." Jones captured or destroyed ship after ship.

When near Flamboro Head, Jones met a fleet of British merchantmen at night, convoyed by the frigate *Serapis*, which was a superior warship to the *Bon Homme Richard*. A withering naval battle ensued in which both ships were set on fire; *Serapis* at least ten times. The *Richard* was riddled with shot, but Jones lashed the two ships together so neither could escape. It was a life or death struggle, one of the most desperate in the annals of naval warfare. At the end of three hours, the British surrendered. The *Richard* was sinking, so Jones transferred his crew to the *Serapis* and sailed away in the prize he had won, while the *Bon Homme Richard* went to the bottom of the sea.

**WASHINGTON'S HEADQUARTERS AT MORRISTOWN**

# FINANCING THE WAR EFFORT

Stalemate tended to underscore the general situation in the United States. The new nation had declared itself independent, but it was occupied by the former colonial power and it was broke. Clearly, the hardships and difficulties were greatly increased because the new nation was without money and without the means of getting a sufficient amount to meet the expenses of the war effort.

The first currency had been issued by Congress in June 1775 and amounted to $2 million. During the war, it would issue $241 million, and the states printed nearly $210 million. These notes, state and national, were only promises to pay, and indeed, the states had no "specie" (gold or silver) to back the notes. In November 1779, Congress voted not to have more than $200 million of paper money in circulation, and issued no more currency. Gold and/or silver would continue to directly back United States currency until 1971.

In the 1770s, however, fear that the colonies might fail in their war for independence, or that they could not redeem the notes even if successful, caused the paper money to be worth less than face value. The British also helped to depreciate the money by putting counterfeit notes in circulation. In 1780 a dollar in coin was worth $40 in paper. The next year the rate was one to $100. It was from this that the expression "not worth a continental" came into use. Dollars were so valueless that people used it for wallpaper in barber shops, for making sailors' clothes, and for other grotesque purposes.

The lack of money caused army officers to seize horses, wagons and supplies throughout the war, giving the owners certificates of value or government currency.

Lack of money brought not only suffering, but mutiny. Because of the want of money, the troops were ragged, hungry, and unpaid. One anonymous essayist wrote: "The severest trial of the Revolution, in fact, was not in the field, where there were shouts to excite and laurels to be won, but in the squalid wretchedness of ill-provided camps, where there was nothing to cheer and everything to endure. To suffer was the lot of the Revolutionary soldier."

Several times the soldiers broke out in open revolt. In 1781, 1,000 men started from Princeton for Philadelphia to demand clothing and back pay. General Clinton sent messengers to invite them to join the British, but the soldiers hung several of these agents who tried to get them to abandon their flag. Happily, order was restored. Lafayette said of the soldiers: "Human patience has its limit. No European army would suffer the tenth part the Americans suffer. It takes citizens to endure hunger, nakedness, toil, and want of pay, which is the condition of our soldiers, the hardiest and most patient that are to be found in the world."

In 1781, Robert Morris (1734-1806), a wealthy Philadelphia merchant, became Superintendent of Finances. Some relief was found through his able management in this period of distress. When no other funds were available, he used his own to support the credit of the nation. Through his efforts, the Bank of North America was established in 1781, and became an aid in securing loans and in carrying on the finances of the nation.

# CAMPAIGNS ON THE SOUTHERN FRONT

During the first three years of the Revolutionary War, most of the action took place in the Northeast, primarily between Boston and Philadelphia. In the latter part of 1778, the British sent a force away from the main field of the war to invade the thinly settled state of Georgia. An army under Colonel Sir John Campbell (1705-1782) sailed from New York while a second force marched from Florida. They captured Savannah in December 1778, and took Augusta early in 1779. By the end of 1779, a royal governor was again placed in charge of the colony of Georgia.

Admiral d'Estaing, commanding the French fleet, along with Polish forces under Count Pulaski and Americans under General Benjamin Lincoln, set out to recapture Savannah in 1779.

After a siege of three weeks, they threw their mobile forces against heavily fortified British positions with heavy losses; their attack withdrew. Among the dead were both Pulaski and d'Estaing. Because the British had made but little progress in the North, their success in

Georgia had encouraged them to transfer the main action of the war to the South. With the aid of a large Tory element, they hoped to take South Carolina, then North Carolina, and move north, subduing one state at a time. In theory, it was a reasonable strategy because it took advantage of the Americans' weakest front.

In 1780 General Clinton and Lord Cornwallis sailed from New York for the South with 8,000 troops. They laid siege to Charleston, which was then the principal city in the South, was defended by an American force under General Lincoln.

After a 48-hour siege and bombardment, Lincoln was forced to surrender on May 12, 1780. The loss of his army of 3,000 troops was a serious blow to the American cause. Hundreds of persons took the oath of allegiance to King George, and it seemed that South Carolina was lost.

In June, Clinton returned to New York with part of the army, leaving Cornwallis in command. Before leaving he wrote: "There are few men in South Carolina who are not either our prisoners or in arms with us."

From Charleston Cornwallis moved northwest across the state, scouring the country, taking the oath of allegiance from the inhabitants, and enlisting Tories to fight with the British.

However, the Continental Congress sent DeKalb with the Maryland and Delaware troops to augment the militia of the Southern states. Washington also sent his Virginia and North Carolina troops. An American army was organized at Hillsboro, North Carolina. General Gates, the "hero of Saratoga," was put in command by Congress, contrary to the wishes of Washington. The army moved forward and confronted Cornwallis at Camden. Here, on August 16, 1780, Gates met the most overwhelming defeat that had yet been suffered by an American army. In fact, his force was practically decimated, but from its remnants and from fresh recruits, a new army was formed at Charlotte under the command of General Nathanael Greene (1742-1786).

In the autumn of 1780, Cornwallis advanced, boasting that he would soon conquer all the states south of the

*ARMED WITH SUPERB KNOWLEDGE OF THE TERRAIN, FRANCIS MARION, KNOWN AS "THE SWAMP FOX," LED GUERRILLA FORCES THAT HARASSED AND EXHAUSTED THE BRITISH IN GEORGIA AND SOUTH CAROLINA.*

Susquehanna River. He sent out side expeditions to "whip the colonists into line." However, the British found themselves advancing into a region where Tories were few and patriot snipers were many. These sharpshooters, all highly skilled the backwoods riflemen, drove the British troops to the top of King's Mountain. On October 7, 1780, they stormed the mountain, killing or capturing the entire British force of 1,100 troops with minimal losses. What Bennington had been in the North, King's Mountain was in the South.

In addition to the regular army, sometimes independent of it, and sometimes working with it, bands of patriot irregulars carried on a merciless guerrilla warfare against the British, particularly in the Southern states. The most

famous of them were Thomas Sumter (1734-1832), Henry "Lighthorse Harry" Lee, Andrew Pickens and Francis Marion (1732-1795), known as "the Swamp Fox."

They were extremely effective because they knew the lay of the land far better than the British forces. They knew every road and path through forest, hills and swamps. There was no telling where a blow from these active, fearless leaders would fall next. From swamp and mountain retreat they struck British outposts, and the rear or flank of an army. They attacked detached parties of British, and inflicted dire punishment on bands of Tories. Their daring and vigilance had much to do with keeping the cause of freedom alive, and in finally recovering the South from the grip of the British.

*GENERAL NATHANAEL GREENE'S CAVALRY OVERWHELMS BRITISH FORCES*

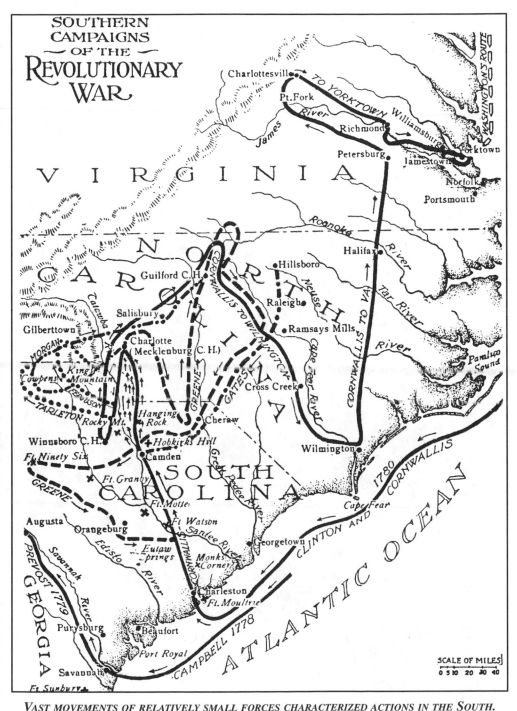

SOUTHERN
CAMPAIGNS
~ OF THE ~
REVOLUTIONARY
WAR

*VAST MOVEMENTS OF RELATIVELY SMALL FORCES CHARACTERIZED ACTIONS IN THE SOUTH.*

After taking command in December 1780, General Greene divided his small army, sending Daniel Morgan (1736-1802) to the southwest to harass Cornwallis and to secure patriot recruits. Cornwallis, however, sent Colonel Banastre Tarleton to dispose of Morgan. The two armies met at Cowpens, South Carolina on January 17, 1781. With superb skill, Morgan gave a crushing defeat to the British, killing, wounding and capturing as many as were in his own command. Tarleton was wounded, but escaped with less than 300 troops. The battle is remembered as one of the brilliant and decisive American victories of the war.

Cornwallis responded to the defeat by hurrying to capture Morgan's army before it could link up with Greene's

*TRAITOR BENEDICT ARNOLD BARELY MISSED BEING SHOT BY A YOUNG WOMAN WHOSE FATHER WAS KILLED BY BRITISH TROOPS UNDER HIS COMMAND.*

force. The three armies raced northward, Morgan closely pursued by Cornwallis, and Greene moving briskly from Cheraw. Morgan escaped across flooded streams to Guilford Court House (now Greensboro), where Greene joined him and took command. They withdrew north into Virginia where they were reinforced.

Greene's strengthened force then returned to North Carolina, and attacked Cornwallis at Guilford Court House on March 15, 1781. Cornwallis held his position, but lost one-third of his army. Patriots rose in force all around him, and only with great difficulty could he get food for his army. Facing these and other dangers, he felt he couldn't risk another battle, so he withdrew to Wilmington, the nearest seaport, for supplies. After resting his army at Wilmington, Cornwallis moved northward into Virginia, where Benedict Arnold, the notorious traitor, was in command of the British forces.

Greene chased Cornwallis for 50 miles after the Battle of Guilford Court House, then turned his attention to recovering South Carolina and Georgia. On April 25, 1781, at Hobkirk's Hill near Camden, he fought an obstinate and indecisive battle with a British force under Lord Rawdon. Aided by "Swamp Fox" Marion, Sumter and Lee, the Americans scurried over the country, taking post after post. The last battle in this region was fought at Eutaw Springs, September 8, 1781. The British were finally driven into Savannah and Charleston, where they could be supported by the guns aboard the warships of their fleet.

Arriving in Virginia, Cornwallis, outranking Benedict Arnold, took command of all the forces. The combined British forces in the state harassed its citizens, destroying large amounts of property, public and private. The opposing French army, under General Lafayette, was too small to offer serious resistance, but active enough to keep the British busy in vain attempts to run it down and capture it. By mid-summer 1781, Lafayette had been sufficiently reinforced to take the offensive.

**GENERAL NATHANAEL GREENE**

57

# VICTORY AT LAST

Though they still held the great ports from New York to Charleston, the British were no closer to beating the Americans in 1781 than they had been in 1776. In fact, the Americans were growing stronger and more determined. The British troops were tired and support in Parliament for continuing the war was weakening. Indeed, the British posture was moving from offensive to merely defensive. Since the Royal Navy had undisputed command of the sea, General Clinton had conceived a strategy of establishing and fortifying coastal positions that could be supplied by sea, and from which troops could be moved as needed.

In the summer of 1781, with this in mind, Clinton told Cornwallis to fortify a coastal position on the Virginia shore to use as such a base. He selected Yorktown, which he began to fortify in August 1781. Lafayette posted his army eight miles away.

Washington was now planning an attack on New York City, which had been weakened by the withdrawal of detachments to the South. A French fleet under Count Jean Baptiste Rochambeau (1725-1807) was to assist. When Washington learned that Cornwallis had taken a defensive position at Yorktown, and that a French fleet, under Admiral Francois de Grasse (1722-1788), would soon sail up the Chesapeake, he changed his plans. Feigning an attack on New York to fool the British, he slipped away on a forced march to Yorktown. He arrived at Philadelphia before Clinton realized that he wasn't attacking New York. From Philadelphia he moved to Elkton, where his troops boarded French ships. They sailed to Williamsburg, Virginia, where they joined Lafayette's army.

By this time, de Grasse's French fleet had sealed off Chesapeake Bay and cut off a potential escape by water. Surrounded by Washington and Lafayette with a combined force of 14,000 French and American troops, the British were hemmed in. Their food supply was cut off, and escape was impossible. Starvation or surrender was the alternative. Clinton sent 7,000 reinforcements to Cornwallis, but it was too late. On October 19, 1781, the day they left New York, Cornwallis surrendered his army of 8,000 troops.

Washington and Lafayette assembled the allied army in two columns over a mile long, facing each other. On the one side were the French, on the other side were the Americans. At the head of one was Washington, at the head of the other was Count Rochambeau. Between these columns the British army marched, with solemn tread, as their drums beat time to the tune "The World Turned Upside Down." Washington directed General Lincoln, who had surrendered to Cornwallis at Charleston, now to receive the sword of Cornwallis.

The news of the surrender of Cornwallis made the colonists wild with delight. A wave of rejoicing swept over the land. When the news reached Philadelphia near midnight, the Liberty Bell rang out, and soon the streets were filled with crowds of happy people. Congress met in a church to give thanks to God, and designated December 13 as a day for national thanksgiving.

When the news of Yorktown reached England, George III's prime minister, Lord Frederick North (1732-1792), said, "Oh, God! It is all over!"

The Revolutionary War was effectively over with the Battle of Yorktown, although it would be two years before the British would finally withdraw from the 13 colonies. Indeed, the King wanted to continue the conflict, but the British people were tired of war. In the spring of 1782, Parliament finally took measures to end it. Clinton was relieved of command. Sir Guy Carleton succeeded him, with instructions to bring the war to a close.

*WASHINGTON'S TROOPS OVERWHELM A BRITISH GUN POSITION AT YORKTOWN*

# THE TREATY OF PARIS

John Adams, Benjamin Franklin and John Jay, as peace commissioners from the United States, met with their English counterparts at Paris to work out the final details of a peace agreement. In November 1782, they agreed on terms, although the treaty was not finally signed until September 3, 1783.

The preliminary treaty was made with Britain without the consent of France, which was in violation of the alliance treaty of 1778. This was because the Americans believed that France wanted to limit the United States to the territory east of the Allegheny Mountains. This would have favored Spain, France's ally against Britain. With this in mind, the Americans secretly induced the British to agree to the Mississippi as the western boundary of the United States. The final treaty was not signed until all the details were agreed upon between France and Spain, as well as England and the United States.

The important provisions of the Treaty of Paris were:

1. Great Britain recognized the independence of the United States as declared on July 4, 1776, and agreed to withdraw all armies, fleets and garrisons with "convenient speed."

2. The United States was given the right to fish off the coasts of Canada and Newfoundland.

3. All debts contracted before the war by merchants of either nation were

**BENJAMIN FRANKLIN**

to be paid. (Nearly all these debts were due to British merchants.)

4. Congress recommended to the state legislatures that they should restore the confiscated property of "real British subjects," and of loyalists who didn't take up arms against the United States, and that they would have a year's time to try to recover their property. Meanwhile, the British government made generous land grants to Tories who would be willing to move to Canada, where they could continue to be British subjects.

5. Each nation, so far as the other was concerned, was to have free navigation of the Mississippi River. (This was for irrelevant at the time, since Spain owned the land on both sides of the mouth of the river, and thus had absolute control of the entrance.)

6. The boundaries of the United States were fixed at the Mississippi on the west; Spanish Florida on the south; and the present boundary on the north.

The 13 colonies, New Hampshire, Massachusetts (incorporating what is now Maine), Rhode Island, Connecticut, New York, New Jersey, Pennsylvania, Maryland, Delaware, Virginia, North Carolina, South Carolina and Georgia, became the first 13 United States. They were joined in 1791 by Vermont, which had been claimed by New Hampshire and New York, and which had proclaimed itself as the Republic of New Connecticut in 1777. A year later, the fifteenth state, Kentucky, which was formed from the territory west of present-day Virginia joined. Tennessee joined as the sixteenth state in 1796.

By a separate treaty, England ceded the Floridas (East Florida and West Florida) to Spain. Spain claimed that West Florida extended as far north as the mouth of the Yazoo River, instead of the 31st parallel. Spain continued to hold the towns in that territory for 12 years. The Floridas were ceded to the United States in 1819, and became the State of Florida in 1845.

The Revolutionary War is estimated to have cost the United States 6,800 troops killed in action, with another 18,500 having died of other causes, particularly due to exposure to the terrible winters. It is very hard to estimate the exact cost of the Revolution, as no official records were kept. It is also hard to adjust for over two centuries of currency fluctuation. The amount spent by England was probably between three and four times that of what was spent by the United States.

As time went on, the British political and military leaders went on to other posts. Charles Cornwallis became a marquis and went on to serve as governor-general in India and as viceroy of Ireland, where he was successful in putting down a rebellion. Sir Henry Clinton served in Parliament and ended his days as governor of Gibraltar. Thomas Gage, recalled after Bunker Hill, stayed in the British army, but slipped into obscurity. Humiliated at Saratoga, John Burgoyne went home a discredited former POW. He resigned from the army briefly, but rejoined to serve as commander-in-chief of forces in Ireland. He later served in Parliament, but retired to become a composer of comic operas.

George III battled his Parliament, syphilis, and bouts with insanity. He would spend the last ten years of his life in the royal equivalent of a padded cell as his son (later George IV) served as prince regent.

On the American side, the leadership went on to somewhat higher levels of greatness. In 1788, George Washington was unanimously elected as the first president of the United States, oversaw the adoption of the Constitution and was re-elected without opposition in 1792. John Adams became the second president in the election of 1796 when Washington refused to run a third time, but lost the 1800 election to another prominent patriot. Having been elected as the third president in 1800, Thomas Jefferson greatly expanded the size of the United States through the Louisiana Purchase in 1803.

Benjamin Franklin, the most prominent of the early leaders not to run for president, served as ambassador to France and helped draft the United States Constitution. Samuel Adams also played a role in drafting the Constitution, and later served as Massachusetts governor. Ethan Allen continued to pursue the idea of an independent Republic of Vermont, but the state eventually became the fourteenth state.

Both Francis Marion and Nathanael Greene retired to their estates in the South. Paul Revere, Boston's favorite silversmith before the war, went back to his metal business, which became a major industry, producing everything from church bells to roofs for public buildings.

The United States survived and prospered, although it would take another war with Britain in 1812-1814 before the former mother country was to finally accept American independence. In the twentieth century, the two nations would bury the bitter rivalries of the past to unite as close allies during and after two world wars.

**GEORGE WASHINGTON DISMISSING HIS GENERAL STAFF AFTER THE WAR**

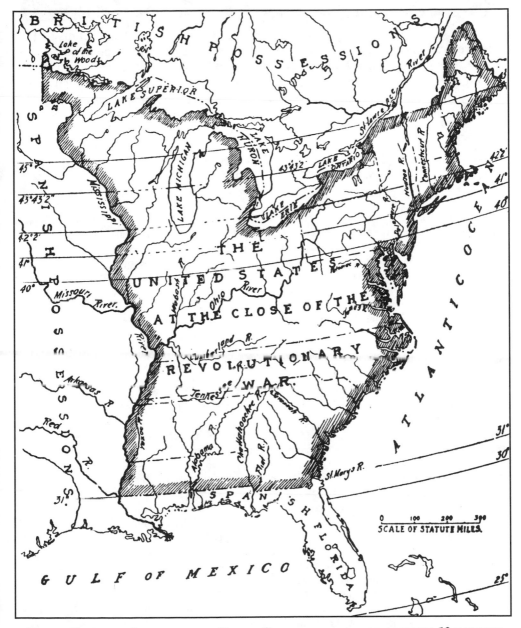

BY THE TREATY OF PARIS, THE NEW UNITED STATES INCLUDED NOT ONLY THE *13* EASTERN
SEABOARD FORMER COLONIES, BUT, THANKS TO THE EFFORTS OF GEORGE ROGERS CLARK,
INCLUDED THE AREA SOUTH OF THE GREAT LAKES AND EXTENDED ALL THE WAY WEST TO THE
MISSISSIPPI RIVER. IN THE NORTH, MAINE WOULD REMAIN AS PART OF MASSACHUSETTS, BUT
VERMONT WAS BRIEFLY AN INDEPENDENT REPUBLIC.

# WHERE TO GO

This section is designed as your guide to parks, historic sites, museums and interpretive centers in the United States and its territories, where you can go to see what life was like during *THE REVOLUTIONARY WAR*.

At these sites, you can see where many of the events in the book actually took place, or view exhibits relating to the everyday lives of the people who lived and worked in America in the period from 1770 to 1783 and beyond.

## 1. Old New-Gate Prison
Newgate Road, East Granby, CT 06026
(203) 653-3563

Colonial America's first copper mine began operations in 1707. During the Revolutionary War it was converted into a prison for Tories and others and in 1776 it became the first state prison in the nation. Visitors can see the old prison buildings, underground caverns and restored guardhouse.

## 2. Old Wethersfield Historic District
505 Silas Deane Highway
Wethersfield, CT 06109

This picturesque New England village contains the oldest restored house in Wethersfield, the 1692 Buttolph-Williams House. Other historic sites include the Silas Deane House, the Isaac Stevens House, and the old meetinghouse. George Washington and the Compte de Rochambeau planned the Yorktown campaign in the Joseph Webb House (1752).

## 3. Dover Division of Historical Affairs
Box 1401
Dover, DE 19903

Dover's green, laid out in 1717, has several handsome homes and the Old State House. Preserved in the Hall of Records are numerous historical documents. The "Penman of the Revolution" lived at the John Dickinson Plantation, where he wrote the stirring words that spurred the patriot cause. The Governor's Mansion reportedly served as an Underground Railroad station.

## 4. National Archives Reference Services
Washington, DC 20408
(202) 501-5400

The National Archives are the nation's historical archives, which include a huge photo collection and numerous research materials.

The original Declaration of Independence, Constitution and the Bill of Rights are displayed in Washington, DC. Regional offices are located in Alaska, California, Colorado, Georgia, Illinois, Massachusetts, Missouri, New York, Pennsylvania, Texas and Washington.

## 5. The Smithsonian Institution
Constitution Avenue
Washington, DC 20560
(202) 357-2700

The Smithsonian is the "nation's attic" and includes numerous museums and galleries, one in Maryland and two in New York. The complex in Washington, DC includes art galleries, museums, and research facilities.

*The National Museum of American History* celebrates American culture and innovations. It exhibits the scientific, cultural, technological and political development of the United States. The collection includes many important artifacts from the Revolutionary War period.

Other Smithsonian facilities in the capital are the *Anacostia Museum, Arthur M. Sackler Gallery, Arts and Industries Building, Freer Gallery of Art, Hirshhorn Museum and Sculpture Garden, John F. Kennedy Center for the Performing Arts, National Air and Space Museum, National Gallery of Art, National Museum of African Art, National Museum of American Art, National*

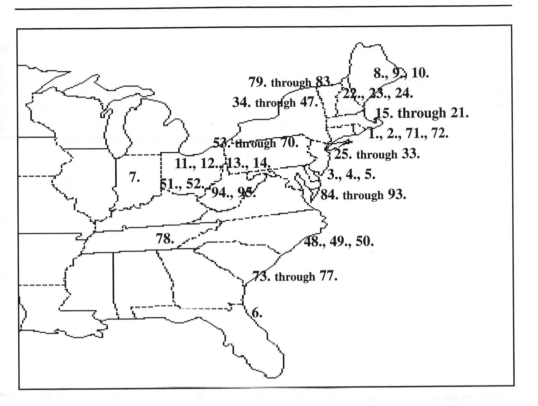

Map labels:
79. through 83.
34. through 47.
8., 9., 10.
22., 23., 24.
15. through 21.
53. through 70.
1., 2., 71., 72.
11., 12., 13., 14.
7.
51., 52.
94., 95.
25. through 33.
3., 4., 5.
84. through 93.
78.
48., 49., 50.
73. through 77.
6.

Museum of Natural History, National Portrait Gallery, National Postal Museum, National Zoological Park, Renwick Gallery, and Smithsonian Institution Building (The Castle).

**6. Castillo de San Marcos National Monument**
Castillo Drive, Avenida Menéndez
St. Augustine, FL 32084
(904) 829-6506

Castillo de San Marcos is the oldest masonry fort and the best preserved example of a Spanish colonial fortification in the continental United States. In 1763, Spain ceded Florida to Great Britain in return for Havana, Cuba. The British held the fort through the American Revolution. In 1783, Florida was returned to Spain, and then in 1821 was ceded to the United States. During the Civil War, Confederate troops briefly occupied the fort. Exhibits trace the long history of the fort.

**7. George Rogers Clark National Historic Park**
401 South Second Street
Vincennes, IN 47591

George Rogers Clark was an imposing figure at six feet two inches tall. As the organizer of the Kentucky militia and commander of its defenses, his military abilities included a knowledge of psychological warfare beyond his peers.' A master of persuasion, he convinced the strategic city of Vincennes, founded by the French, to support the American revolutionaries. With the French and their allies, the Native Americans, Clark's victories in the Northwest decided the future of the Northwestern Territories. The park features the George Rogers Clark Memorial Building (1931).

**8. Maine State Museum**
State House Complex
Library/Archives Building
Augusta, ME 04330
(207) 289-2301

The museum features exhibits pertaining to Maine's natural resources, social history and industrial heritage. The "Made in Maine" collection of 19th century manufacturing equipment and related displays, which include a textile factory and a water-powered woodworking mill, is of special interest. The museum also displays a collection of artifacts recovered from the sunken Revolutionary War privateer DEFENCE.

### 9. Dyer Library and York Institute Museum
371 & 375 Main Street, Saco, ME 04072
(207) 282-3031 or 283-3861

The library, located in the 19th century Deering House, maintains a 500 volume collection on Maine history. It also includes photographs, documents and family papers, city records and furniture by Otto Lange. The museum, founded in 1867, features a colonial kitchen, Empire and 18th century clocks and paintings by American artists, including John Brewster, Jr. Also exhibited are artifacts, clothing and furniture of the Revolutionary War period. Both the library and the museum feature art galleries.

### 10. York Village
The Old York Historical Society
York, ME 03909

Displayed in York are the Elizabeth Perkins House; the Emerson-Wilcox House (1740); the Old York Gaol (1719), restored to its 1790 appearance; the reconstructed and restored Jefferds Tavern; and the John Hancock Warehouse, once owned by that signer of the Declaration of Independence.

### 11. Annapolis Historic District
652 Main Street
Annapolis, MD 21401

Annapolis was the nation's capitol for a short time after the Revolution. Many restored buildings are open to the public, including the Hammond-Harwood House (1774). The State House is the nation's oldest in continuous use. In addition, the US Naval Academy (1845) houses a museum of naval history.

### 12. Fort McHenry National Monument
Baltimore, MD 21230

Fort McHenry was hastily erected in 1776 by Patriots to defend Baltimore from the British navy. In the 1790s a permanent installation was built, serving for 100 years. During the War of 1812, the fort was bombarded for 25 hours before the British gave up. It was this long night and American victory that inspired Francis Scott Key to write "The Star Spangled Banner." Visitors can tour the fort's batteries, barracks, and bastions.

### 13. Fort Washington Park
Indian Head Highway
Ft. Washington, MD 20021

The first fort, built in 1809 to protect the new nation's capitol, was destroyed during the War of 1812. It was replaced in 1824 and now offers daily tours, featuring military demonstrations on Sundays.

### 14. Frederick Visitor Information Center
19 East Church Street
Frederick, MD 21701

Frederick, in 1765, was the first to rebel against the Stamp Act. During the Civil War, the town paid a $200,000 ransom to the Confederate General Jubal Early to avoid being burned. Visitors can see historic buildings, including the Rose Hill Manor, Barbara Fritchie home and glove shop, and Roger Brooke Taney home.

### 15. Boston National Historic Park, The Freedom Trail and the Bunker Hill Monument
Boston, MA 02205

Within the context of the Boston National Historic Park, the US National Park Service preserves many of the essential buildings and landmarks where the important events of 1775-1776 occurred. *The Freedom Trail* is a walking trail that winds through historic Boston, beginning at Boston Common near the Massachusetts State House. Among the many sites included are *Faneuil Hall*, the *Old North Church*, *Paul Revere's Home* and the *Bunker Hill Monument*.

### 16. Christ Church National Historic Landmark
City Hall, 795 Massachusetts Avenue
Cambridge, MA 02139

Built in 1761, the church was used as a barracks by the colonial soldiers, and its organ pipes were melted down for bullets. At Christmas, 1775, the church reopened for services, which George and Martha Washington attended. The church and the Waterhouse House (1753) are the only two original buildings left facing the Common. Upon the Common is a bronze tablet which marks the spot where, on July 3, 1775, Washington is supposed to have taken command of the Continental forces.

### 17. Minute Man National Historic Park
Box 160, Concord, MA 01742
(508) 369-6993

The 750-acre park stretches along the British route from Lexington and Concord, commemorating the beginning of the Revolutionary War. Among the sites within the park are: the Battle Road Visitor Center; the North Bridge, where "the shot heard 'round the world" was fired in April 1775; the North Bridge Visitor Center; the Wayside, the home of the muster master of the Concord Militia; Meriam's Corner; Hardy's Hill; Bloody Angles; Hartwell Tavern; Captain William Smith House; Paul Revere Capture Site; and the Fiske House Site.

### 18. The Concord Museum
Jct. of Cambridge Turnpike and Lexington Road
Concord, MA 01742
(508) 369-9609

The museum exhibits Native American artifacts, items from the Revolutionary war, Paul Revere's lantern, Ralph Waldo Emerson's personal effects from his study, Thoreau's belongings from Walden Pond, furniture, and decorative arts.

### 19. Historic Deerfield
Deerfield, MA 01342
(413) 774-5581

This complex of 12 historic homes includes: Allen House (1720), Ashley House, Barnard

Tavern (early 1800s), Dwight House (1725), Ebenezer Hinsdale and Anna Williams House (restored to its 1813-1838 appearance), Frary House (1700s, restored in 1890), Helen Geier Flynt Textile Museum, Henry Needham Flynt Silver and Metalware Collection, Sheldon-Hawkes House, Stebbins House, Wells-Thorn House (1725 to 1850 period rooms), and Wright House (1824).

### 20. St. Michael's Church
26 Pleasant Street, Marblehead, MA 01945
(617) 631-0657

Built in 1714 with materials brought from England, the church is one of the oldest Episcopal churches in America. Its bell was rung at the news of the Declaration of Independence until it cracked. Recast by Paul Revere, it is still in use.

### 21. Springfield Armory National Historic Site
One Armory Square, Springfield, MA 01105

Established in 1777, the first US arsenal stored muskets, cannon and other weapons and produced paper cartridges. In 1794, President Washington selected Springfield as the site of a Federal Armory. By 1819 the armory had become the center of invention and development of new weaponry. Today, the Springfield Armory National Historic Site includes 55 acres and several buildings of the original armory complex. The main attraction is the Main Arsenal Building (c. 1840s), which holds the world's largest collection of small arms. Other buildings on the grounds are the Commanding Officer's Quarters and the Master Armorer's House.

### 22. Old Fort No. 4
Charlestown, NH 03630

Begun in 1746, this fort was successfully defended only three years later against a large force of French and Native Americans. In 1777 General John Stark gathered his troops here before their victory at Bennington, Vermont. Reconstructed buildings include the Great Hall, watchtower, stockade, and barns.

### 23. Dartmouth College
The Green, Hanover, NH 03755
(603) 646-2900, 646-2422 or 643-5672

Founded in 1769 by Reverend Eleazar Wheelock, the campus has grown to include many colonial and modern structures. They include the Baker Memorial Library (1928), the Hood Museum of Art, the Hopkins Center for the Creative and Performing Arts and the Webster Cottage (1780).

### 24. Portsmouth Trail
500 Market Street, Portsmouth, NH 03801
(603) 436-1118

Tickets and tour maps are available at the Chamber of Commerce. The tour of historic buildings include: *the Governor John Langdon House* (1784), *the John Paul Jones House* (1758), *the Moffatt-Ladd House* (1763), *the Rundlet-May House* (1807), *the Warner House* (1716) and *the Wentworth-Gardner House* (1760).

### 25. Boxwood Hall Historic Site
1073 East Jersey Street, Elizabeth, NJ 07201
(201) 648-4540

Boxwood Hall (c. 1750), also known as Boudinot Mansion, once housed Elias Boudinot, a president of the Continental Congress and signer of the Treaty of Peace with Great Britain. George Washington visited the mansion on April 23, 1789, while en route to his presidential inauguration in New York City.

### 26. Fort Lee Historic Park
Hudson Terrace, south of the George Washington Bridge, Fort Lee, NJ 07024
(201) 461-1776

Built in 1776 by George Washington's troops, Fort Lee was a major link in the fortifications defending New York and the Hudson River against British warships. The park features a visitor center with displays and models, reconstructed cannon batteries and a rifle parapet.

### 27. Monmouth Battlefield State Park
SR 33, Freehold, NJ 07728
(908) 462-9616

This park was the site of one of the largest and longest Revolutionary War battles, fought on June 28, 1778. The visitor center features displays that trace and explain the troops movements during the battle. Also on the grounds are the Craig House (1710), used by the British as a field hospital, and Owl Haven, a nature center.

### 28. Steuben House State Historic Site
(Ackerman-Zabriskie-Steuben House)
1209 Main Street, Hackensack, NJ 07601
(201) 487-1739

The 1713 house displays the museum collection of the Bergen County Historical Society and 1650-1850 Jersey Dutch furnishings. The house was also General George Washington's headquarters in 1780.

### 29. Batsto Historic Site
Route 542, Hammonton, NJ 08037
(609) 561-3262

Founded in 1766, the Batsto Iron Works became an important ironmaking center and a supplier of munitions for the American army during the Revolutionary War and the War of 1812. The iron furnaces shut down in 1848 but the community continued to produce window glass until 1867. The restored village features a Victorian mansion, sawmill, workers' cottages, gristmill, blacksmith and wheelwright shops, general store, and the oldest known operating post office in the United States.

### 30. Morristown National Historic Park
Morristown, NJ 07960

Only 30 miles from British-held New York City, General Washington and his army endured mutiny, sickness, and starvation in this hamlet. The Washingtons spent the harsh winter of 1779-1780 at the Ford Mansion, now preserved and furnished with period pieces. The museum has exhibits on 19th century items and weapons. Historical sites include Fort Nonsense, Jockey Hollow, and the Wick House, which served as the headquarters of Major General Arthur St. Clair.

### 31. Waterloo Village Restoration
Route 206, near Netcong, NJ 07857

During the Revolution this busy village, known as Andover Forge, furnished the Continental army with musket barrels and cannonballs. It is now a group of restored Early American buildings dating back to 1760, including the church, apothecary, smithy, carriage house, stagecoach inn, gristmill, general store and craft shops.

### 32. Dey Mansion
199 Totowa Road
Preakness Valley Park, NJ 07470
(201) 696-1776

The 1740 brick and brownstone Georgian house displays antiques and items from the 18th century in both the detached kitchen and main house. General George Washington also used the house for his headquarters in July, October and November of 1780.

### 33. Trenton
Mercer County Chamber of Commerce
214 West State Street, Trenton, NJ 08607
(609) 393-4143

Trenton has a long history, founded in 1680 with the building of a mill at the falls of the Delaware River. Its potential for industry was recognized, and by 1719 the village had grown dramatically. Today Trenton remains a major industrial center for the Northeast. Historic sites include the New Jersey State Museum, the Old Barracks Museum (1758), the State House (1792), the Trent House (1719) and the Washington Crossing State Park.

### 34. The Erie Canal/Oriskany Battlefield
NY Department of Transportation
1220 Washington Avenue, Albany, NY 12232

Mules and horses towed wooden barges along the 363 mile long canal that linked Albany with Buffalo. "Clinton's Folly" speeded trade and settlement of the old Northwest. The original locks can be seen at Fort Hunter, west of Amsterdam, and at Lockport. Near Rome is the Oriskany Battlefield, scene of a Revolutionary War battle.

### 35. Schuyler Mansion State Historic Site
32 Catherine Street, Albany, NY 12202
(518) 434-0834

The Schuyler Mansion was the home of the noted Revolutionary War general and US senator from New York, Philip Schuyler. His daughter Betsy married Alexander Hamilton in the house.

### 36. Senate House State Historic Site
312 Fair Street, Kingston, NY 12401
(914) 338-2786

This was the first meeting place of the first New York State Senate, at the Abraham Van Gaasbeek home. Rooms are furnished as they would have appeared in 1777. A museum features Hudson Valley furnishings and art exhibits relating to Hudson Valley artists, including John Vanderlyn.

### 37. St. Paul's National Historic Site
897 S. Columbus Avenue
Mount Vernon, NY 10550
(914) 667-4116

St. Paul's Church was established in the 17th century, and the present building was built in 1787. The village green next to the church was the setting for events linked with John Peter Zenger's fight for freedom of the press. The Bill of Rights Museum occupies the former parish hall.

### 38. Washington's Headquarters State Historic Site
Liberty at Washington, Newburgh, NY 12550
(914) 562-1195

The Hasbrouck House (1750) was General George Washington's headquarters from April 1782 until August 1783. The nearby museum contains exhibits about the Continental Army. The six-acre park includes the Tower of Victory monument (1887).

### 39. Federal Hall National Monument
26 Wall Street, New York, NY 10005

The government of the United States of America began to function on Wednesday, March 4, 1789, at this spot, in New York's City Hall. Renamed

Federal Hall in honor of its new importance, this was the first capitol. The federal government moved to Philadelphia in 1790, and to Washington, DC in 1800. By this time the Federal Hall was too small to serve the city government's needs and construction of a new City Hall began. In 1812, the crumbling Federal Building was sold for salvage. The US Customs Building (1842) now occupies the site.

## 40. Hamilton Grange
New York Group, National Park Service
26 Wall Street, New York, NY 10005

Born in the West Indies in 1755, Alexander Hamilton was sent to New York for his education, by a Presbyterian minister and several other leading citizens of St. Croix Island. An ambitious man, Hamilton became involved in the Revolutionary effort, becoming one of its military leaders. Hamilton also pressed for the emancipation of slaves, enlisting in the Continental Army and the eventual abolishment of slavery. Although he continued to hold slaves himself, he was a founding member of the New York Society for the Manumission of Slaves. Hamilton Grange is the country estate that he built for his wife, Elizabeth, and their five children. Eventually, the house will be restored to its mid-eighteenth century appearance. Today visitors find an interpretive program planned around the themes of drama, music and colonial crafts.

## 41. New York Historical Society
170 Central Park West at 77th Street
New York, NY 10024
(212) 873-3400

The historical society houses a museum, print room and reference library. Its collections focus upon American history, New York history, American fine arts and the decorative arts.

## 42. New York Public Library
42nd St. at Fifth Avenue, New York, NY 10017
(212) 930-0800

The public library features more than five million volumes in its research library, including specialized collections of American history.

## 43. Fort Stanwix National Monument
112 East Park Street, Rome, NY 13440
(315) 336-2090

Originally built in 1758, Fort Stanwix has been almost completely reconstructed to its 1777 appearance. The British began a two pronged attack down the Mohawk Valley, General Barry St. Leger invading from the west and General John Burgoyne from the north. St. Leger besieged the fort on August 3, 1777. The eventual lifting of the British siege on August 22 led directly to Burgoyne's surrender two months later at Saratoga. This was considered to be a turning point of the Revolution, leading to the formal French, Dutch, and Spanish alliances that helped win America's independence. Today the monument features a storehouse, bombproof barracks and casemates. Exhibits at the museum depict the history of the upper Mohawk Valley. The park is on a tour and living history schedule for most of the year.

## 44. Saratoga National Historic Park
648 Route 32, Stillwater, NY 12170-1604

"The turning point of the American Revolution," this 2,700 acre park commemorates the defeat of the British by colonial forces in 1777. This battle encouraged France to help America. An auto and walking tour includes the Freeman Farm Overlook, the Neilson Farm, the American river fortifications, the Chatfield Farm, the Barber wheat field, the Balcarres Redoubt, the Breymann Redoubt, General Burgoyne's Headquarters, the Great Redoubt, and the Fraser Burial Site and Trail. Visitors can also see the Schuyler House and the Saratoga Monument.

## 45. Fort Ticonderoga
Route 74, Ticonderoga, NY 12883

Reconstructed to the original 1755 French plans, the fort features a parade ground, bastions, barracks, ramparts, a well-marked battlefield around the fort and a museum. The fort was first called Fort Carillon by the French and, after its capture in 1759 by the British, renamed Ticonderoga. During the Revolution, the fort fell to Ethan Allen's Green Mountain Boys.

## 46. Knox's Headquarters State Historic Site
Forge Hill Road, Vail's Gate, NY 12584
(914) 561-5498

The John Ellison home served as headquarters for three Revolutionary War generals: Nathanael Greene, Henry Knox and Horatio Gates. The house is furnished in period and costumed historians give interpretive programs of the 50-acre site. Also on the grounds are the remains of the Ellison grist mill.

## 47. The United States Military Academy
West Point, NY 10996

Exhibits at the West Point Museum trace the history of the Academy, established in 1802 by Congress to train military officers. The site was a vital fort during the Revolutionary War and also displays a monument dedicated to Civil War soldiers.

## 48. Moores Creek National Battlefield
PO Box 69, Currie, NC 28435

Early in 1776 the Tories and the patriots fought here in a brief but crucial battle. The rout of the British forces, including a battalion of Highland Scots, prevented a meeting with the British ships at the coast, and galvanized the population into supporting the patriots' cause and conducting the first vote for independence.
Earthworks and monuments can be seen on the walking tour, including the Patriot (Grady) Monument, the Loyalist Monument, the James Moore Monument, and one honoring the women of Lower Cape Fear, who helped win victory.

## 49. Edenton Historic District
116 East King Street, Edenton, NC 27932

Nearly 50 historic sites are preserved in this town, founded in 1712 but not named until 1722. The Chowan County Courthouse (1767) is the oldest in use in the state. Nearby is the Teapot Memorial, commemorating the 51 women who gathered on the courthouse green in 1774, forswearing the drinking of tea and the wearing of English garments.

## 50. Guilford Courthouse
## National Military Park
PO Box 9806, Greensboro, NC 27429

This is where Lord Cornwallis' troops beat General Nathanael Greene's militia on March 15, 1781. However, the British suffered such heavy losses that they were unable to press on with the offensive. Explaining the battle that eventually led to Cornwallis' surrender seven months later at Yorktown, Virginia, are markers, monuments, a film and exhibits. The self guiding tour features the sites of the American first line, American second line, last shots by American riflemen, Washington's cavalry charge, site of the Guilford Courthouse, American third line, and the Greene Monument.

## 51. Fort Laurens State Memorial and Museum
West of Junction 1-77 and SR 212
Bolivar, OH 44612
(216) 874-2059

During the American Revolution, this 81 acre park was the site of the only US military fort in Ohio. Revolutionary War displays are exhibited in the museum and an audiovisual presentation explains the history of the fort.

## 52. Schoenbrunn Village State Memorial
SR 259, New Philadelphia, OH
(216) 339-3636

Founded in 1772 as a Moravian mission to the Delaware Indians, Schoenbrunn was the first settlement in Ohio. In 1777 British and American hostilities led to the town's abandonment and it was later destroyed. Today the village features the mission cemetery, 17 reconstructed log buildings and 2 1/2 acres of planted fields.

## 53. Sun Inn
564 Main Street, Bethlehem, PA 18018
(215) 866-1758

The Sun Inn, established in 1758 as a way station for colonial statesmen like George Washington, the Marquis de Lafayette and John Adams, is fully restored and furnished in period.

### 54. Harriton House

1 1/4 miles north of US 30 on Morris Avenue,
then 1/2 mile west on Old Gulph Road,
then north on Harriton Road to the entrance
Bryn Mawr, PA 19010
(610) 525-0201

Built in 1704, the two story stone house was the
home of Charles Thomson, secretary of the
Continental Congress. The house has been
restored and has some of its original furnishings.

### 55. Peter Wentz Farmstead

3/10 mile southeast of Junction SR 73 and 363
Center Point, PA 19474
(610) 584-5104

This 18th century working farm features a
Georgian-style mansion furnished in period, live-
stock, a German kitchen garden, apple orchards,
craft and farming demonstrations and a slide presentation. The house was also used twice as
George Washington's headquarters during the
Revolutionary War.

### 56. Brandywine Battlefield State Historic Park

US 1, Chadds Ford, PA 19317

Philadelphia was left open to the advancing
British troops after General George Washington's
defeat at the Battle of the Brandywine on
September 11, 1777. The 50 acre park includes
Lafayette's quarters and the reconstructed head-
quarters of Washington. Nearby are the John
Chadd House, Birmingham Friends Meeting
House, and the Brinton House (1704).

### 57. Cornwall Iron Furnace

off US 322, 4 miles north of I-76 off SR 72 on SR
419, in Cornwall, PA 17016
(717) 272-9711

Built in 1742 by Peter Grubb, the furnace operated until 1883, producing stoves, kitchenware and
farm tools, as well as cannons and ammunition for
the Continental Army. Structures include: the
original furnace stack, the blast machinery, blow-
ing tubs, wagon and blacksmith shops, the open
pit mine, the ironmaster's mansion, and the
Charcoal House.

### 58. Mercer Museum

Pine at Ashland Street, Doylestown, PA 18901
(215) 345-0210

Exhibits trace the pre-industrial history of the
nation from colonization to the Civil War. More
than 60 crafts and trades are represented by artifacts and implements from the 18th and 19th centuries.

### 59. Hopewell Furnace National Historic Site

Route 1, Box 345, Elverson, PA 19520
(610) 582-8773

The Hopewell Furnace was built on French Creek
by Mark Bird in 1771. The furnace cast pig iron,
hollowware, stoves, and other items. During the
Revolutionary War it produced cannon and shot.
It operated until 1883, when it became unprof-
itable. Visitors can see the restored and refur-
nished ironmaster's mansion, tenant houses,
water wheel, blast machinery, bridge house, cool-
ing shed, barn, store, and the ruin of an 1853
anthracite furnace which has been stabilized. The
visitor center features an audiovisual program and
exhibits with original castings produced at
Hopewell Furnace and tools used in 18th and 19th
century iron making.

### 60. Historic Fallsington

4 Yardley Avenue, Fallsington, PA 19054
(215) 295-6567

Visitors can see the town nearly as it was when
Quaker William Penn worshiped here 300 years
ago. The homes range from Pennsylvania's first
log cabins to Victorian mansions. Restored buildings on Meetinghouse Square include an 18th
century inn, the Burges-Lippincott House (1789),
and three Friends meeting houses.

### 61. Lancaster

Pennsylvania Dutch Convention and Visitors
Bureau, 501 Greenfield Road
Lancaster, PA 17601
(717) 299-8901 or (800) 723-8824

Lancaster was the largest inland city in the
colonies during the Revolutionary War. It was
also the capitol of the nation for one day when

Congress, while fleeing Philadelphia after the Battle of Brandywine, stopped in the city. Historic and cultural sites in the city include the Amish Farm and House, the Hans Herr House (1719), the Landis Valley Museum, Mill Bridge Village and Wheatland, the former home of James Buchanan, the 15th President of the United States.

## 62. Philadelphia Convention and Visitors Center
16th Street and John F. Kennedy Boulevard
Philadelphia, PA 19102
(215) 636-1666 or (800) 537-7676

The United States was born in Philadelphia on July 4, 1776, in Independence Hall. The Constitution was drafted there in September 1787, laying the framework for the nation's future. Today, visitors can see the Afro-American Historical and Cultural Museum, the Army-Navy Museum, the Atwater Kent Museum, The History Museum of Philadelphia, the Betsy Ross House, City Hall, the Civil War Library and Museum, Congress Hall, the Fairmount Park Historic Houses, Independence Hall, the United States Mint and the Liberty Bell.
*(See following entry).*

## 63. Independence National Historical Park
313 Walnut Street
Philadelphia, PA 19106

Philadelphia is where the First Continental Congress met in 1774, airing their grievances against King George III. Within the park, visitors can see the Betsy Ross House, the Bishop White House, the Carpenters' Hall, Christ Church (c. 1730s), the Christ Church Cemetery, Congress Hall, the Declaration House, the First Bank of the United States, Franklin Court, the Free Quaker Meeting House (1783), Independence Hall, Independence Square, the Liberty Bell, the Mikveh Israel Cemetery, the Old City Hall, the Philadelphia Exchange, the Philosophical Hall, St. George's Church (1769), St. Joseph's Church, the Thaddeus Kosciusko National Memorial and the Todd House.

## 64. Deshler-Morris House
5442 Germantown Ave., Philadelphia, PA 19144

This 1750s home was built by the German immigrant David Deshler, after he had become a prosperous Philadelphia Quaker merchant. During the Revolutionary War, the Deshler-Morris House was used briefly as a headquarters by the British Commander, Sir William Howe. It was leased by President George Washington in 1793 when a yellow fever epidemic raged through Philadelphia.

## 65. Pittsburgh Convention & Visitors Bureau
4 Gateway Center, Suite 514
Pittsburgh, PA 15222
(412) 281-7711 or (800) 359-0758

The site of Pittsburgh was selected by George Washington during the Revolutionary War. Pittsburgh grew rapidly and plunged into America's industrial age. Interesting sites in the city include the Allegheny Observatory, the Carnegie Library of Pittsburgh, the Historical Society of Western Pennsylvania, the Pittsburgh Children's Museum, the Point State Park and the Soldiers and Sailors Memorial Hall.

## 66. Valley Forge National Historical Park
Valley Forge, PA 19481

Remains of fortifications and reconstructed soldiers' huts dot the 3,000 acre park, the site where General Washington's army bivouacked through the bitter winter of 1777-1778. Three thousand of the tattered, starving soldiers died, but the survivors emerged a rejuvenated and determined army. Also on this site are Washington's Headquarters, the quarters of General Varnum, the Washington Memorial Chapel, a museum, and Mill Grove, the first American home of John James Audubon (1785-1851).

## 67. The Chester County Historical Society
225 North High Street
West Chester, PA 19380
(610) 692-4800

The historical society displays early American furniture and decorative arts, including clocks, ceramics, crystal and silver. The changing exhibits feature clothing, textiles, dolls and ceramics. It also maintains a research library which focuses upon genealogy and area history.

**68. Lycoming County Historical Museum**
858 West Fourth St., Williamsport, PA 17701
(717) 326-3326

The museum features artifacts ranging from 10,000 BC, to the early Native American cultures and the arrival of the European settlers. Among the exhibits are a blacksmith shop, a carpenter shop, a Victorian parlor, a gristmill and a Shempp toy train collection.

**69. Washington Crossing State Park**
Washington Crossing, PA 18977

On Christmas night 1776, George Washington and 2,400 soldiers crossed the Delaware in a blinding snowstorm to attack Hessian mercenaries in Trenton, New Jersey. The 500 acres of the park are divided into two areas. The northern area, the Bowman Hill Wildflower Preserve, includes Bowman's Hill Tower, Memorial Flagstaff, and the Thompson-Neely House (1702). The southern area, the Washington Crossing Section, includes the McConkey Ferry Inn (1750s), Memorial Building, and the Taylor House (1816). A reenactment of the crossing of the Delaware is held at 1 pm on December 25.

**70. Historical Society of York County Museum**
250 East Market Street, York, PA 17403

The Historical Society's museum contains exhibits showing life in York up to the 20th century and a genealogical library. The charm of colonial York is captured here, on the Street of Shops and village square. Also on Market Street is the Bonham House, Golden Plough Tavern (1740s), Bobb Log House (1812), and the General Gates House. The General Gates House was the scene of the Conway Cabal conspiracy, where Lafayette prevented the overthrow of General Washington as head of the Continental Army.

**71. Hunter House**
54 Washington Street, Newport, RI 02840
(401) 847-1000

Built in 1748 by Jonathan Nichols, the Deputy Governor of Rhode Island, the restored house is an outstanding example of colonial architecture.

It features 18th century furniture, paneling, paintings, silver and a colonial garden. It served as the headquarters of Admiral de Ternay, commander of the French naval forces during the Revolutionary War.

**72. Redwood Library and Athenaeum**
50 Bellevue Drive, Newport, RI 02840
(401) 847-0292

Built in 1748-1750, the library contains many old and valuable books. It also has a collection of early 18th and 19th century portraits, including seven by Gilbert Stuart.

**73. Historic Camden**
Camden, SC 29020

Revolutionary War battles raged in this town founded by Irish Quakers in 1750. Most of the town was burned by the British troops as they departed in 1781. The Cornwallis House was used as a headquarters by the British general. A restored area features the reconstructed remains of British forts.

**74. Cowpens National Battlefield**
PO Box 308, Chesnee, SC 29323

On January 17, 1781, the patriots commanded by Brig. Gen. Daniel Morgan fought a superior British force led by Lt. Col. Banastre Tarleton. In this key Revolutionary War battle, Morgan turned retreat into victory by turning his troops to face, stand and fire point blank into the pursuing redcoats. Featured at the park is a visitor center with exhibits, a tour road, and a walking trail through the heart of the battlefield.

**75. Kings Mountain National Military Park**
PO Box 40, Kings Mountain, SC 28086

The Revolutionary War did not affect the remote settlements east of the Alleghenies until 1780, when the British began a conquest of the South. The mountain men formed regiments and used guerrilla warfare against the redcoats, ending in a vicious battle on October 7 at this site. The battle, won by the patriots, is described by exhibits, monuments, and markers throughout the 4,000 acre park. A foot trail meanders over the battle-field.

## 76. Ninety Six National Historic Site
US 248, Ninety Six, SC 29666

This frontier post was founded in 1751 by Robert Gouedy, who opened a store. He built a huge trade, growing grain and tobacco, raising cattle, serving as a banker, and selling cloth, shoes, beads, gunpowder, tools, and rum. By the time of the Revolution, the town of Ninety Six contained 12 houses, a courthouse, a jail and was surrounded by a stockade. On November 18, 1775, the first major land battle in the South began with 1,800 loyalists attacking the 600 patriots at Ninety Six. Even after a truce was declared, the patriot spirit was running high and a savage war of factions continued until 1781. Visitors can see the historic Island Ford Road, siege lines, the Star Fort, the site of Ninety Six, the jail site, the stockade fort, and the site of the village of Cambridge.

## 77. Fort Moultrie
### Fort Sumter National Monument
Drawer R, Sullivans Island, SC 29482

Fort Moultrie was not completed when Admiral Sir Peter Parker and nine warships attacked on June 28, 1776. After a nine hour battle the ships retired. Charleston was saved from British occupation and the fort was named after its commander, William Moultrie. The British did capture the fort in 1780 and abandoned it after the Revolutionary War was over. A second Fort Moultrie was built in 1798 and destroyed by a hurricane in 1804. A third fort was built by 1809. During the Civil War, the Confederates held Fort Moultrie against the Union forces until Charleston was evacuated in 1865. In the 1870s Fort Moultrie was modernized. By both World Wars, the old fort had become only a small part of the fortifications and weaponry that covered most of the island. Today visitors move backwards through time from the World War II Harbor Entrance Control Post to the reconstructed section of the palmetto-log fort of 1776.

## 78. Knoxville Visitors Bureau
Box 15012, Knoxville, TN 37901

Knoxville was founded after the Revolutionary War as a repair and supply center for westbound wagon trains. During the Civil War the town was badly damaged. Within the city are several historic sites and monuments, including: the restored Gen. James White's Fort, built by the first white settler, with a main house, three log cabins and stockade; Marble Springs Historic Farm National Historic Landmark; Blount Mansion National Historic Landmark (1792); Ramsey House National Historic Site; and Bleak House, used as a headquarters by Confederate General James Longstreet, which is now a museum of Southern history.

## 79. Bennington Chamber of Commerce
Veterans Memorial Drive,
Bennington, VT 05201

The restored Old First Church has been restored to its early 1700s appearance. Its cemetery contains the graves of soldiers who died in the Battle of Bennington in 1777 and the poet Robert Frost. The Bennington Museum displays a collection of Grandma Moses paintings and Early American memorabilia. It also operates the restored Peter Matteson Tavern in Shaftsbury.

## 80. Hubbardton Battlefield and Museum
East Hubbardton,
Castleton, VT 05735
(802) 828-3226

The only Revolutionary War battle fought in Vermont was located seven miles north of US 4 at East Hubbardton. On July 7, 1777, colonial troops retreating from Fort Ticonderoga turned and repelled the pursuing British and German forces. An electric relief map and a diorama show the battle.

## 81. Montpelier State Capitol
State Street, Montpelier, VT 05602

The capitol building is an impressive Doric style. Built of Barre granite, the structure features a gilded dome surmounted by a statue of Ceres, the goddess of agriculture. Inside stands a brass cannon captured from the Hessians in the Battle of Bennington (1777) and a statue of Ethan Allen.

## 82. The Vermont Museum
Pavilion Office Building, 109 State Street
Montpelier, VT 05602
(802) 828-2291

The museum traces the history of Vermont, from the Native Americans to the present. Changing exhibitions feature different historical themes.

## 83. Shelburne Museum and Heritage Park
US 7
Shelburne, VT 05482
(802) 985-3344

The park is a collection of 37 restored buildings, many dismantled and moved to the park, housing collections of art, artifacts and memorabilia depicting early New England life. Some of the structures are furnished 18th and 19th century houses, a jail, country store, schoolhouse, stage-coach inn, apothecary, blacksmith shop and railroad depot. Other attractions include a double lane covered bridge, round barn, locomotive and private car, a model circus parade more than 500 feet long and the 1906 sidewheeler S.S. *Ticonderoga*. The museum features many varied collections focusing upon Americana.

## 84. Charlottesville Historic District
Visitors Bureau, Box 161
Charlottesville, VA 22902

Thomas Jefferson exerted a major influence upon the architecture of Charlottesville. He founded and designed the University of Virginia in 1819. Nearby is James Monroe's country estate, Ash Lawn, and Jefferson's own mansion.

## 85. Hugh Mercer Apothecary Shop
Caroline and Amelia streets
Fredericksburg, VA 22401
(703) 373-3362

Opened in 1761, the apothecary features a drug room with curious bottles, ancient showcases and yellowed ledgers; a sitting room; and a small library used by George Washington as an office. Demonstrations of 18th century medical practices include leeching, cupping, bleeding and herbal remedies.

## 86. St. George's Church
Princess Anne and George streets
Fredericksburg, VA 22401
(703) 373-4133

This Episcopal church was built in 1732, and the current building dates from 1849. It contains three original L.C. Tiffany windows and a memorial window to Mary Washington. Buried in the churchyard are William Paul, the brother of John Paul Jones, and John Dandridge of New Kent, the father of Martha Washington.

## 87. Gunston Hall Plantation
Lorton, VA 22079
(703) 550-9220

Gunston Hall (1755) was built by George Mason, author of the Virginia Declaration of Rights of 1776 and one of the writers of the US Constitution. Designed by William Buckland, the house features woodcarvings and English and American furnishings. On the grounds are out-buildings, including the dairy, kitchen, laundry, smokehouse, and schoolhouse and formal 18th century style gardens.

## 88. Monticello
Thomas Jefferson Memorial Foundation
Monticello, VA 22902

This imposing mansion was designed by Thomas Jefferson and was his home from 1769 to 1826.

## 89. St. Paul's Church
St. Paul Boulevard and City Hall Avenue
Norfolk, VA 23510
(804) 627-4353

Built in 1739 upon the site of a 1641 church known as the "Chapel of Ease," St. Paul's Episcopalian Church was the only building left after the burning of Norfolk in 1776. A cannonball fired from a British ship remains imbedded in its wall. Graves in the cemetery date from the 17th century.

## 90. St. John's Episcopal Church
24th at Broad Street, Richmond, VA 23223
(804) 648-5015

Built in 1741, this is the site where Patrick Henry made his stirring speech in favor of independence.

## 91. George Washington Birthplace National Monument

RR 1, Box 717
Washington's Birthplace, VA 22443
(804) 224-1732

The monument is located on the Potomac River, 38 miles east of Fredericksburg, VA and is accessible via Va. 3 and Va. 204. The site itself is a recreation of 18th century Popes Creek Plantation. Park facilities include the historic birthplace home area, colonial farm, burial ground, hiking trails, beach and picnic area.

## 92. Colonial National Historical Park Jamestown and Yorktown

P.O. Box 210
Yorktown, VA 23690
(804) 898-3400

Jamestown and Yorktown, located on the Virginia Peninsula, between the James and York rivers, are two eminent places in American history. Thanks to the 23 mile long Colonial Parkway it is easy to follow the sequence of history, from the colonial beginnings at Jamestown to the winning of national independence at Yorktown.

## 93. Mount Vernon

Mount Vernon, VA 22121

George Washington's estate on the Potomac River has been restored to its 1799 appearance. This is where the Washington family settled in 1738 and George and Martha raised her two children after their marriage in 1759.

Visitors can see the mansion and museum, filled with many original furnishings; the bed where Washington died; his sword; the key to the Bastille, presented by the Marquis de Lafayette; and personal mementos of Martha Washington and her granddaughter Nelly Custis.

Preserved on the grounds are the stables, kitchen, gardens, rebuilt greenhouses and slave quarters, and tomb of George and Martha Washington. The site has been preserved for posterity by an organi-zation called the Mount Vernon Ladies' Association.

## 94. Point Pleasant Battle Monument State Park

Tu-Endie-Wei Park,
Point Pleasant, WV 25550
(304) 675-3330

On October 10, 1774, Virginia frontiersmen defeated Chief Cornstalk and the Shawnee in the final battle of Lord Dunsmore's War.

This campaign to subdue the Native Americans was begun by Lord Dunsmore, who goaded the Indians into attacking General Andrew Lewis and the frontiersmen. His goal was to end the frontiersmen's involvement in the Revolutionary cause.

This battle is believed to have been the opening engagement of the American Revolution. An 84 foot high granite shaft with a statue of a typical Virginia woodsman at its base commemorates the battle. Also within the park is the grave of "Mad Anne" Bailey, a legendary female soldier and border scout.

## 95. Fort New Salem

Salem, WV 26426

Divided loyalties during the Revolutionary War split the Seventh Day Baptist Church of Salem, New Jersey. In 1792, 72 members of the congregation left to build a new home in the wilderness. Reconstructed by Salem College, the fifteen original log buildings serve as living museums, craft workshops, and college classrooms to study frontier life.

*Please note:* While we have made every effort to insure the accuracy of the information in this section, certain data such as, but not limited to, phone numbers and mailing addresses, is subject to change.

It is always best to plan your visit well in advance and to call ahead for hours and availability.

# INDEX

under study is stimulated by application of an electric current.

**Embolism**—The sudden blockage of an artery by a clot or abnormal particle (such as an air bubble) circulating in the blood.

**Embryo**—The developing human individual from the time of implantation to the end of the eighth week after conception.

**Endemic**—Disease that is constantly present in a community or group of people. Endemic disease may affect only a few people at any one time.

**Endocrine System**—System of organs that secrete hormones into the blood to regulate basic functions of cells and tissues. The endocrine organs are the anterior and posterior pituitary glands, thyroid and parathyroid glands, pancreas, adrenal glands, ovaries (in women) and testicles (in men).

**Endocrinologist**—Doctor specially trained in diagnosis and treatment of endocrine disorders.

**Endometrial Biopsy**—A biopsy of the endometrium.

**Endometrial Cancer**—Cancer of the endometrium.

**Endometriosis**—A condition in which functioning endometrial tissue occurs in places within the pelvic cavity other than the uterus, and often results in severe pain and infertility.

**Endometritis**—Inflammation of the endometrium.

**Endometrium**—The mucous membrane lining of the uterus.

**Endomyometritis**—Inflammation of the muscular substance (or myometrium) of the uterus.

**Endoscopy**—Method of diagnosing diseases in hollow organs. An endoscope (an optical instrument with a lighted tip) is inserted into the organ, which allows visual examination of the cavity. Used in the abdomen, pelvis, lumen of the bronchial tubes or intestines.

**Endotracheal Tube**—Tube temporarily placed in the trachea (windpipe) of patients who are unable to breathe normally because of disease or surgery.

**Enteric**—Relating to the small intestine. Enteric-coated medicine is coated with a hard shell that dissolves when it reaches the small intestine.

**Enteroscopy**—Examination of the inside of the intestines with an endoscope, an optical instrument.

**Enterostomy**—Surgically created artificial opening for elimination of feces. An enterostomy nurse or enterostomy specialist is a professional who teaches patients how to care for the artificial opening.

**Enzymes**—Proteins manufactured by the body that regulate the rate of essential life processes (metabolism).

**Epinephrine**—Same as *Adrenalin*.

**Episcleritis**—Inflammation of tissues on the sclera (the white of the eye).

**Episiotomy**—Surgical enlargement of the vulvar orifice for obstetrical purposes, usually during childbirth.

**Epithelial Horn**—Thick, rough lesion protruding from the skin. It may become cancerous if not removed.

**Equine Virus**—Virus that causes a serious form of encephalitis in horses and humans.

**Ergot**—Medication derived from a fungus that grows on rye plant. It is used to treat migraine headache and to increase strength of uterine contractions during and immediately after childbirth.

**Esophageal Varices**—Enlarged veins on the lining of the esophagus. They are subject to severe bleeding and often appear in patients with severe liver disease.

**Esophagoscopy**—Method of diagnosing diseases of the esophagus by means of an esophagoscope, an optical instrument with lenses and a lighted tip.

**Esophagus**—Muscular tube connecting the throat and stomach.

**Estrogen**—Female sex hormone, primarily secreted by the ovaries. It can also be produced synthetically for use in estrogen replacement therapy.

**Estrogen Receptor Value**—Used in the study of breast-cancer cells to determine the best treatment.

**Etiology**—Cause or causes of a disease.

**Eustachian Tubes**—Slender passages between the throat and the middle ear that maintain normal air pressure in the middle ear.

**Excise**—To remove by excision.

**Excision**—Surgical removal or resection of a diseased part.

**Exploratory Laparotomy**—Diagnosing abdominal disease by surgically opening the abdomen and examining its contents.

**Extremities**—Arms and legs.

**Eye Bank**—Facility where living corneas are stored and made available for transplantation.

**Eyes, Crossed**—Condition in which muscles controlling the eyes are unbalanced. The eyes point in different directions. Also called squint or strabismus.

# F

**Fallopian Tubes**—Organs of the female reproductive tract through which an egg (ovum) passes from the ovary to the uterus. Tying these tubes (tubal ligation) accomplishes sterility.

**Familial Polyposis**—Inherited condition in which the lining of the intestines contains many polyps, some of which may become cancerous.

**Family History**—Information about illnesses that tend to occur within a family. This information is used to determine the likelihood of diseases occurring in other members of the family.

**Farsightedness**—Same as *Hypermetropia*.

**Fascia**—Sheet or band of tough, fibrous tissue that covers muscles and other body organs.

**Fecal**—Relating to feces, waste products eliminated through the lower intestinal tract.

**Fecal-Oral**—Pathway by which some fecal germs gain entry into the bloodstream. Sewage in drinking water, hand-to-mouth transmission after bowel movements or sexual contact can cause infection.

**Feces**—Body waste formed of undigested food that has passed through the gastrointestinal system to the colon. Feces are produced and stored in the colon until eliminated.

**Fertilization**—An act or process of insemination or impregnation, as when a sperm penetrates an egg.

**Fetal**—Of, relating to or being a fetus.

**Fetal Monitoring**—Measuring the heart rate of the fetus during labor.

**Fetal-Scalp Electrodes**—Fine wires attached to the scalp of a fetus to measure heart rate and rhythm during labor.

**Fetal-Scalp Monitoring**—Measuring the well-being of the fetus during labor by obtaining blood from the scalp or by measuring the heart rate of the fetus or contraction strength of the uterus.

**Fetus**—A developing human from usually three months after conception to birth.

**Fever**—Above-normal body temperature. Normal mouth temperature is 98.6F (37C). Normal rectal temperature is 99.6F (37.6C).

**Fiber**—A non-nutritious ingredient of many complex carbohydrates. Fiber increases bulk in the diet. Many nutritionists recommend including ample fiber in the diet. Experimental studies and clinical studies show that people who eat high-fiber diets are less likely to develop colon cancer, diverticulitis, atherosclerosis and gallbladder disease.

**Fiber Optics**—System of transmitting light and images through thread-like strands of glass. Fiber-optic instruments make some examinations and surgical procedures simple, safe and effective.

**Fibrin**—Protein formed by the action of blood clotting on fibrinogen.

**Fibrinogen**—Protein in the blood needed for blood clotting.

**Fibrositis**—Inflammatory conditions affecting connective tissue of muscles, joints, ligaments and tendons.

**First Molars**—First permanent flat teeth, used for grinding food, which appear at about age 6 to 7.

**Fissure**—Break in the skin or inner lining of organs.

**Fistula**—Abnormal passage between two organs or between the body and the outside.

**Flank**—Area on the side of the body below the ribs and above the hip.

**Fleas**—Tiny biting insects. Most cause minor skin irritation; some carry and transmit serious diseases such as plague and typhus.

**Flooding**—A drastic form of psychotherapy used for treatment of phobias. A patient is suddenly confronted with the feared object or placed in the feared situation with no chance of escape. Having experienced the

chromosomes of cells. Genes transmit inherited characteristics such as eye color, blood type, gender or body shape. Defective genes cause many kinds of birth defects and inborn diseases.

**Gene, Dominant or Recessive**—Dominant gene, if present in either the mother's egg or father's sperm, will transmit its characteristics to the newborn child. Recessive gene must be present in both parents before its characteristic will be transmitted.

**General Surgeon**—A doctor specially trained to perform operations.

**Genetic Counseling**—Counseling to help couples decide whether to have children or not when there is a risk of genetic disease being transmitted to the child.

**Genetics**—Science of determining inherited factors that result in the unique make-up of every human being; also, science that traces the appearance patterns to genetic (inherited) disease.

**Genitourinary Tract**—Body system that forms, stores and eliminates urine. Also has a role in male and female reproductive functions. Organs include the kidneys, ureters, bladder, urethra, uterus, fallopian tubes, ovaries, vagina, cervix, penis, scrotum and testicles.

**Germs**—Organisms that cause infection, such as bacteria, viruses or fungi.

**Gestation**—Time spent in the mother's uterus by the fetus. Average gestation time for the human infant, from conception to delivery, is approximately 39 weeks.

**Gigantism**—Condition in which the body or a body part grows excessively, sometimes due to an overactive pituitary gland.

**Glucagon**—Hormone secreted by the pancreas that increases blood sugar. A synthetic form is sometimes used as emergency treatment for patients with diabetes who have temporarily low blood sugar.

**Glucose**—Major form of sugar in the blood, stored primarily in the liver. It provides energy to most tissues, organs and systems.

**Glucose-Tolerance Test**—Method of diagnosing diabetes mellitus or functional hypoglycemia. The patient drinks a measured amount of glucose (sugar). The blood and urine are tested at measured intervals for glucose content.

**Gluten**—Protein found in wheat and other foods that cannot be digested by some persons because of genetic disease. A gluten-free diet allows persons with the disorder to digest food and grow normally.

**Glycosuria**—Sugar in the urine.

**Gonads**—Parts of the reproductive system that produce and release female eggs (ovaries) or male sperm (testes).

**Growth Disorders**—Conditions in children that result in underdevelopment or overdevelopment of the body. Diseases of the endocrine glands, nutritional problems or genetic abnormalities are frequently the causes.

**G Spot**—A small area of sensitive tissue that some women identify on the vaginal wall which, when stimulated, can provide intense sexual arousal and pleasure.

**Gynecologist**—Doctor specially trained to treat diseases of the female reproductive system.

# H

**H-2 Blocker Drugs**—Class of antihistamines that reduce the production of stomach acid for treatment of peptic ulcers.

**Hallucinogens**—Substances that produce hallucinations, apparent sights, sounds or other experiences that do not actually exist.

**Hand Surgeon**—Surgeon specially trained to treat hand diseases, injuries, infections and arthritic conditions.

**Hangover**—Unpleasant aftereffects of excessive consumption of alcoholic beverages. Symptoms include irritability, headache and nausea. Sometimes, the same feelings result from using certain medications.

**Hashimoto's Thyroiditis**—One of several kinds of inflammation of the thyroid gland.

**Heart Catheterization**—Same as *Cardiac Catheterization.*

**Heart-Lung Machine**—Complex mechanical device that provides artificial function of a patient's heart and lungs for a short time during open-heart surgery and heart or lung transplantation.

**Heart Tumors**—Rare tumors that grow in the heart wall or in the heart chambers, interfering with normal heart function.

**Hemangioma**—A usually benign tumor made up of blood vessels that typically occurs as a purplish or reddish, slightly elevated area of skin.

**Hematocrit**—Blood test used to detect anemia and other blood disorders. It is expressed as the percentage of blood made up of red blood cells (remainder of the blood is made up of serum or plasma). Normal hematocrit range is approximately 35% to 45%, but it varies with age and sex.

**Hematologist**—Doctor specially trained to diagnose and treat diseases of the blood and blood-forming organs.

**Hemochromatosis**—Disease in which excessive iron accumulates in the liver, pancreas and skin, resulting in liver disease, diabetes mellitus and a bronzed skin color.

**Hemoglobin, Hemoglobin Range**—1) Component that carries oxygen to body tissues. 2) Blood test used to detect anemia and other blood disorders, expressed in grams per 100 cubic centimeters. The normal hemoglobin range is approximately 12 to 18 grams per 100 cubic centimeters and varies according to age and sex.

**Heterosexual**—1) Pertaining to the opposite sex. 2) A person who is sexually attracted to members of the opposite sex.

**High Blood Pressure**—See *Hypertension*.

**Hirschsprung's Disease**—Congenital defect of infants in which the colon cannot eliminate feces, resulting in severe constipation.

**Hirsutism**—Excessive growth of hair in a normal or abnormal distribution, especially in women.

**Histamine**—Chemical in body tissues that dilates the smallest blood vessels, constricts the muscle around the bronchial tubes, stimulates stomach secretions and produces an allergic response.

**HIV**—See *Human Immunodeficiency Virus*.

**Holter Monitor**—Instrument that detects heartbeat-rhythm abnormalities for 24 hours or longer. The device is portable for patients to carry wherever they go.

**Homosexual**—1) Pertaining to the same sex. 2) A person who is sexually attracted to a person of the same sex.

**Homosexuality**—Sexual and emotional attraction to members of one's own sex.

**Hormones**—Powerful substances manufactured by the endocrine glands and carried by the blood to body tissues and organs. Hormones determine growth and structure of many organs (such as during growth and maturation) and also control many vital body functions.

**Host**—Person or animal with an infection that has been received from another person, animal or plant, or the environment.

**Human Immunodeficiency Virus (HIV)**—Any of a group of retroviruses that infect and destroy helper T cells of the immune system and weaken the body's natural abilities to fight infections and cancer. Also called the AIDS virus.

**Hyaline-Membrane Disease**—Serious condition of premature infants in which the lungs can't expand normally. Cause is unknown.

**Hydatidiform Mole**—Disease occurring during early pregnancy, resulting in death of the fetus and an overgrowth of tissue within the uterus.

**Hydramnios and Polyhydramnios**—Condition in which amniotic fluid (fluid in the uterus that surrounds the fetus until birth) becomes excessive.

**Hygiene**—Personal self-care and cleanliness that reduces the risk of infections and diseases.

**Hyoid Bone**—V-shaped bone located just above the larynx.

**Hyperalimentation**—Method of supplying total nutritional needs of patients unable to eat normally. The method (usually intravenous or by tube through the nose into the stomach) provides nutrients containing essential proteins, fats, carbohydrates and vitamins.

**Hyperbaric Chamber**—Large, sealed room in which air pressure can be raised above normal levels. It is used primarily to treat patients with either decompression sickness or severe burns (sometimes).

**Hyperbilirubinemia**—The presence of an excess of bilirubin (a reddish-yellow pigment) in the blood.

**Hypercalcemia**—Presence of excessive calcium in the blood, occasionally a sign of malignancy.

**Hyperlipoproteinemia**—Condition in which excessive lipoproteins (cholesterol and other fatty materials) accumulate in the blood.

**Hypermetropia**—Seeing distant objects clearly while nearby objects appear blurred; also called farsightedness.

**Hypersensitivity**—Extreme sensitivity to any agent (drugs, pollens, chemicals, etc.) that causes allergic reactions. Some reactions can be life-threatening, but most are less serious.

**Hypertension**—1) Abnormally high arterial blood pressure. 2) A systemic condition resulting from hypertension that is either symptomless or is accompanied by headache, dizziness or nervousness.

**Hypnotics**—Medications that produce sleep.

**Hypocalcemia**—A deficiency of calcium in the blood.

**Hypochondriasis**—Mental illness in which a person is convinced that serious disease is present, despite examination that proves otherwise. The symptoms of the imagined disease seem real to the patient (often called a hypochondriac).

**Hypogammaglobulinemia**—An immunologically deficient state characterized by an abnormally low level of all classes of gamma globulin in the blood.

**Hypoglycemia**—An abnormal decrease of sugar in the blood.

**Hypoplastic Anemia (Aplastic Anemia)**—Group of anemias that decrease blood-producing bone marrow. This can be life-threatening.

**Hypothalamus**—Part of the brain that regulates body functions such as temperature, blood pressure, appetite and thirst.

**Hysterectomy**—Surgical removal of the uterus.

**Hysteria**—1) Condition in which a person becomes anxious and excitable and experiences impaired sensory and motor abilities. Sometimes, hysterical persons simulate conditions of diseases such as deafness or blindness. 2) Outbreak of uncontrolled emotions, such as fits of laughing or crying.

**Hysterogram**—An x-ray of the uterus.

**Hysterosalpingogram**—An x-ray photograph made by hysterosalpingography.

**Hysterosalpingography**—Studying the uterus and fallopian tubes by injecting material into the uterus that x-rays can detect. It is used primarily to determine if the passageway for the ovum (egg) is open all the way to the uterus. The x-ray image is the hysterosalpingogram.

**Hysteroscope**—An instrument with lens system and lighted tip used in direct visual examination of the cervix and cavity of the uterus.

**Hysteroscopy**—Inspection of the cervix and/or uterus with a hysteroscope.

**Hysterotomy**—Surgical incision of the uterus.

# I

**I-131 Uptake**—Measuring thyroid activity with radioactive iodine and radiation emission counters.

**Idiopathic**—Arising spontaneously or from an obscure or unknown cause.

**Ileum**—Part of the small intestine just above the large intestine (colon).

**Ileus**—Condition of the small intestine in which either an obstruction or paralysis prevents material from passing through the intestine.

**Iliac Arteries**—Large arteries in the inner pelvis that supply blood to the legs.

**Immune, Immunity**—Resistance or protection against infection by the body's natural defenses. A person may be immune to one kind of infection but not immune to another. Some infections, such as measles, chickenpox or mumps, cause the body to become immune permanently to that infection.

**Immune System**—Body's system of defense against infection.

**Immunization**—Producing immunity by giving a vaccine (orally or by injection) of germs that have been altered so they cannot produce significant disease. The vaccine causes the body's immune system to produce antibodies that create immunity.

**Immunosuppressants**—Drugs used in immunosuppression treatment to weaken the immune system and to inhibit immune response.

**Immunosuppression**—Prevention of the body from forming a normal immune response. It is used to treat diseases (especially when organs must be transplanted) when certain antibodies must be inactivated.

**Impotence**—Male's inability to achieve or sustain an erection or to ejaculate sperm during sexual intercourse.

**Incise, Incision**—To cut open or cut into.

**Incomplete Abortion**—Abortion in which the uterus is not entirely rid of its contents.

**Incomplete Spontaneous Miscarriage**—Naturally occurring miscarriage in which the fetus is expelled, but part of the placenta remains in the uterus. Excessive bleeding and infection can result unless the uterus is emptied, usually by dilatation and curettage of the uterus (D & C) or suction curettage.

**Incubation Period**—The time between exposure to an infecting germ and the appearance of symptoms indicating an infection. Also describes the period of bacterial growth in laboratory cultures.

**Induced Abortion**—Abortion brought on intentionally.

**Infant**—Child between the ages of 2 weeks and 1 year.

**Infection, Infectious**—Disease caused by germs (bacteria, viruses, fungi) that enter the body and cause inflammation or other processes that have an adverse effect on health.

**Infertility**—Inability to produce offspring.

**Inflammation, Inflammatory Process**—Process by which the body attempts to overcome illness-producing causes such as germs, injuries such as burns, or diseases such as arthritis. The process causes increased body heat (fever or local warmth), swelling, pain and tenderness. If the inflammation is near the skin, redness results.

**Ingestion**—Taking in food, medicine, etc., by mouth.

**Inhalation**—Breathing air into the lungs.

**Inherited**—Body characteristic that is transmitted from one generation to the next by chromosomes in the mother's egg and father's sperm. Some inherited characteristics such as brown eyes are normal; others such as Down syndrome are disorders.

**Inoculation**—Injection of infected material such as pus into a nutrient medium where the germs will grow, or incubate. They are then stained and analyzed through a microscope. Also describes any kind of immunization.

**Insufflation Test**—See *Rubin's Insufflation Test.*

**Insulin**—Hormone produced by the pancreas that helps regulate sugar in the blood and helps produce energy.

**Intensive Care Unit (ICU)**—Area of a hospital where patients who are seriously ill or recovering from serious surgery are given more care than is available in other hospital units. As soon as the condition improves, the patient is transferred from the ICU to a regular hospital unit.

**Intermittent**—Happening only occasionally or under certain conditions.

**Internist**—Doctor specially trained in nonsurgical diagnosis and treatment of diseases in adults.

**Intervertebral Disk**—Cartilage that connects adjacent vertebrae in the spinal column.

**Intestinal Tract**—All parts of the gastrointestinal tract except the mouth, esophagus and stomach. The intestinal tract organs are duodenum, small bowel, ileum, cecum, appendix, ascending colon, transverse colon, descending colon, sigmoid colon, rectum and anus.

**Intestine, Large**—Last major portion of the gastrointestinal tract located just under the small intestine. It is also called the colon or large bowel. It processes waste material into feces, which are stored until eliminated from the body.

**Intestine, Small**—Longest section of the gastrointestinal tract, located just under the stomach and duodenum. It absorbs digested food into the bloodstream and passes waste material into the large intestine.

**Intracytoplasmic Sperm Injection (ICSI)**— A method of in-vitro fertilization whereby a single sperm is injected into a single egg and the resulting zygote is transferred to the uterus.

**Intrauterine**—Of, situated in, used in or occurring within the uterus. Also, involving or occurring during the part of development that takes place in the uterus.

**Intrauterine Death**—Death of a fetus while inside the mother's uterus.

**Intrauterine Device (IUD)**—Birth control method in which a small device is inserted and left in the uterus to prevent growth of fertilized eggs.

**Intrauterine Growth Retardation (IUGR)**—A condition in which a fetus is much smaller than would be expected for its gestational age. Contrary to the name, babies who are diagnosed with IUGR usually do not have any physical or mental retardation after birth, and suffer from growth retardation only while in the womb.

**Intravenous**—Within the vein. Fluids, medications and nutrients that cannot be taken orally are given intravenously by a needle placed in a large vein near the surface of the skin.

**Intravenous Pyelogram (IVP)**—See *Pyelogram, Intravenous*.

**Intravenous Urography**—Method of studying the kidneys and urinary tract by injecting into the bloodstream a medication that x-rays can detect.

**In-vitro Fertilization (IVF)**—Procedure in which eggs from the female are harvested, impregnated in the lab with sperm from the male and implanted in the uterus.

**IQ (Intelligence Quotient)**—Supposedly a measure of a person's intelligence, rather than what one has learned. Recent research on intelligence raises questions about the accuracy and meaning of the IQ test.

**Iridectomy**—Surgery performed to treat some kinds of glaucoma.

**Iron-deficiency Anemia**—An anemia that is caused by a deficiency of iron and is characterized by a deficiency of hemoglobin in the red blood cells.

**Irrigation**—Flooding with water or other liquid. It is used frequently to clean wounds or areas of the body that will undergo surgery.

**Isolation, Reverse Isolation**—Procedures to prevent spread of infection in a hospital. Isolation protects hospital staff and visitors from contracting a contagious disease from a patient. Reverse isolation protects a patient susceptible to infection because of immunosuppression from contracting infection from hospital staff or visitors.

**IUD**—See *Intrauterine Device*.

**IUGR**—See *Intrauterine Growth Retardation*.

**IVP**—See *Pyelogram, Intravenous*.

## J

**Jaundice**—Yellow skin and whites of the eyes, dark urine and light stools, symptoms of diseases of the liver and blood.

**Joint**—Structure that enables two or more bones to move easily in relation to each other. A joint consists of ligaments and cartilage that hold bones together.

**Joint Capsule**—Tough, fibrous tissue that surrounds a joint.

**Joint Replacement**—Replacement of diseased joints with mechanical joints. The wrist, hip and knee joints are among the most common joints replaced.

## K

**Karyotype**—The chromosomal characteristics of a cell. Also, the chromosomes themselves or a representation of them.

**Karyotyping**—To determine the genetic charcteristics of a newborn infant with a suspected genetic anomaly.

**Kegel Exercises (Kegels)**—Repetitive contractions by a woman of the muscles that are used to stop the urinary flow in urination in order to increase the tone of the pubic muscles, especially to control incontinence or to enhance sexual responsiveness.

**Ketoacidosis**—Serious complication of diabetes mellitus in which the body produces acids that cause fluid and electrolyte disorders, dehydration and sometimes coma.

## L

**Labor**—The physical activities involved in giving birth, consisting essentially of a prolonged series of involuntary contractions of the uterine muscles, together with both reflex and voluntary contractions of the abdominal wall. Also, the period of time during which such labor takes place.

**Laboratory**—A place equipped for

experimental study in a science or for testing and analysis.

**Labor Room**—A hospital room where a woman in labor stays before being taken to the delivery room. In some hospitals, labor and delivery will both occur in the same room.

**Laceration**—Wound with jagged edges.

**Lactiferous Ducts**—Network of tubes in the female breast that collects milk and delivers it to the nipple.

**Laminaria**—Freeze-dried seaweed sometimes used to dilate the cervix when performing an abortion.

**Laparoscopy**—Exploratory examination of the organs inside the abdominal cavity with a laparoscope, an optical instrument with a lighted tip. The laparoscope is inserted into the abdomen through a small incision. Visual examination can then be made of many abdominal organs.

**Laparotomy**—Exploratory surgery in the abdomen performed to diagnose and sometimes treat abdominal disease.

**Laryngeal Nerve**—Nerve located in the neck that controls the vocal cords and enables a person to speak.

**Laryngoscopy**—Examination of the inside of the larynx with a laryngoscope, an optical instrument.

**Larynx**—Structure of muscle and cartilage in the upper neck. It contains the vocal cords. Air passes through the larynx into the windpipe and then into the lungs. The "Adam's apple" is part of the larynx.

**Laser Therapy**—Using a laser beam to treat many diseases. Sharply focused laser light creates intense heat and is valuable in cutting tissue, destroying unwanted tissue and joining tissue together. It is most often used to treat retinal detachment, endometriosis or atherosclerosis.

**Latent**—Present but inactive; something that exists in an undeveloped form.

**Laxatives**—Medications used to treat constipation.

**Leboyer Birth**—Method of childbirth designed to reduce trauma for the newborn by avoiding the use of forceps and bright lights in the delivery room and by giving the newborn a warm bath. Named for Frederick Leboyer, a French obstetrician who began to question Western methods of childbirth after visiting India in 1958. Dissatisfied with modern delivery room techniques, he advocated a series of procedures that included dimmed lighting, soft sounds, gentle massaging of the infant, a delayed severing of the umbilical cord and a warm-water bath.

**Lesbian**—A woman who is sexually attracted to other women.

**Lesion**—General term for injury or damage to an organ or tissue.

**Lethargy**—Fatigue or lack of usual physical or mental energy.

**Libido**—Sexual desire.

**Life Cycle**—Growth and development from birth to death.

**Ligaments**—Strong, flexible cords of tissue near joints that hold bones together and permit bone motion.

**Lipoproteins (High Density and Low Density)**—Components of the fluid in blood that are measured to help predict the likelihood of atherosclerosis (hardening of the arteries).

**Liposuction**—A surgical removal of localized fat deposits (as in the thighs or buttocks), especially for cosmetic purposes, by applying suction through a small tube inserted in the body.

**Liquid Nitrogen**—Nitrogen that has been cooled until it becomes a liquid. It is used most often in cryosurgery.

**Local Anesthesia**—See *Anesthesia, Local.*

**Lower GI Series**—Same as *Barium X-rays.*

**Low-Residue Diet**—Diet consisting of foods that are digested almost entirely, leaving minimal material to form feces.

**Low-Spinal Anesthesia**—Also called "saddle-block" anesthesia. An injection into the lower spinal canal provides anesthesia to the lower body.

**Lumbar Puncture (Spinal Tap)**—A diagnostic procedure in which a needle is inserted between 2 bones (vertebrae) of the lower spine to collect spinal fluid for laboratory examination.

**Lumbar Spine**—Lower part of the spine, from the lowest ribs to the bottom of the spine.

**Lymphangiogram, Lymphangiography**—Diagnostic method of studying the lymphatic system by injecting a material into the lymph channels that x-rays can detect. The image on x-ray film is the lymphangiogram.

**Lymphatic Leukemia**—Class of leukemias, involving primarily lymphatic cells, affecting children and adults.

**Lymph Channels**—Tubes of tissue that carry lymph fluid away from tissues and back to the bloodstream. Lymph fluid is composed of proteins and water, varying in composition in different parts of the body.

**Lymph Glands**—Small collections of tissue (nodes) located along lymph channels in areas such as the elbow, armpit or groin. When infection is present, nearby lymph glands enlarge, become tender and destroy germs that enter lymph channels. Lymph glands also manufacture antibodies to help fight infection.

**Lymphocytes**—One of several types of white blood cells that help fight infection.

**Lymph (or Lymphatic) System**—Lymph channels and lymph glands considered as a single body system.

**Lymphosarcoma**—Class of cancers of the lymphatic system.

# M

**Macular Degeneration of the Eye**—Condition of the macula (area on the retina that provides detailed vision) in which impaired blood supply causes gradual vision loss.

**Macule**—General term for any discolored spot or patch on the skin, such as a freckle.

**Magnetic Resonance Imaging**—See *MRI*.

**Malignant**—Capable of causing great harm, including death. It usually refers to cancerous growth.

**Mammogram, Mammography**—Diagnostic method of studying the female breast by an x-ray technique that detects cancerous growths while they are still treatable. The image on x-ray film is the mammogram.

**Manic-Depressive Illness**—Mental illness in which behavior alternates between unrealistic enthusiasm and deep depression.

**Manometry**—The measuring of pressure (of either liquid or gas) by means of a manometer.

**MAO Inhibitors**—See *Monoamine Oxidase Inhibitors*.

**Marijuana**—Mood-altering substance that is usually taken into the body by smoking. It is derived from Indian hemp or cannabis leaves, stems and seed pods.

**Marrow**—Core of many bones, where most of the body's blood cells are produced.

**Mastoiditis**—Infection of the mastoid (bony area just behind the ear).

**Masturbation**—Erotic stimulation, especially of one's own genitals, commonly resulting in orgasm.

**Maternal**—Pertaining to, related through or inherited from the mother.

**Maternal-Fetal Medicine Specialist**—An obstetrician-gynecologist who has received subspecialized training in the treatment of high-risk pregnancies, including maternal and fetal complications.

**Mediators**—Substances that 1) help nerve impulses travel from one cell to the next, 2) participate in the allergic process.

**Medic Alert**—Nonprofit agency that maintains a medical-record system. Subscribers receive a bracelet or pendant that states their medical condition and provides a toll-free number for more information. The service can save the life of a person with a major medical condition who may not be able to provide medical history. For information write: Medic Alert Foundation, P.O. Box 1009, Turlock, CA 95381; (800) 344-3226.

**Medical History**—Essential facts about past and present medical conditions. Knowing your medical history enables your doctor to plan the best possible health care. Carry a card stating essential health details in your purse or wallet, and consider joining the Medic-Alert program (see above).

**Meibomian Glands**—Small glands on the inner eyelid. They secrete a fluid that helps the eyelids move easily over the surface of the eye.

**Membrane**—Thin tissue lining a body cavity, covering an internal organ or dividing a space.

**Meninges**—Three-layered membrane covering the brain.

**Menopause**—The period of natural cessation of a woman's menstrual cycle that normally occurs between the ages of 40 and 55.

**Menorrhagia**—Abnormally heavy menstrual flow.

**Menorrhea**—Normal menstrual flow.

**Menses**—The menstrual flow.

**Menstrual**—Of or relating to menstruation.

**Menstrual Cycle**—The whole cycle of physiological changes in a woman's body from the beginning of one menstrual period to the beginning of the next.

**Menstruate**—To discharge blood from the genital tract at monthly intervals.

**Menstruation**—A discharging of blood, secretions and tissue debris from the uterus that recurs at approximately four-week intervals in nonpregnant women of reproductive age.

**Mental System (Mind)**—Functions of the brain that provide the abilities to perceive surroundings, to have emotions, imagination, memory, will and to process information.

**Metastases**—Cancerous cells or infectious germs that spread from their original location to other parts of the body.

**Metatarsal Bones**—Bones in the middle of the foot.

**Midwife**—Nurse with special training and experience in childbirth.

**Minilaparotomy**—A ligation (tying) of the fallopian tubes through a small incision in the abdominal wall.

**Miscarriage**—Spontaneous explusion of a human fetus before it is viable, especially between the 12th and 28th weeks of gestation.

**Miscarry**—To suffer miscarriage of a fetus.

**Misdiagnose**—To diagnose incorrectly.

**Missed Abortion**—An intrauterine death of a fetus that is not followed by its immediate expulsion.

**Mole**—Skin lesion, often dark-brown or black.

**Monoamine Oxidase (MAO) Inhibitors**—Medications used to treat some forms of depression.

**Monogamous**—See *Monogamy*.

**Monogamy**—The state or custom of being married to only one person at a time or of having only one mate at a time.

**Motor Nerve**—Nerve that transmits the stimulus that causes muscles to contract.

**MRI (Magnetic Resonance Imaging)**—A method of studying the body's internal structures that employs a strong magnetic field (rather than x-rays) and a computer to produce detailed pictures.

**Mucous Membrane**—Thin tissue lining internal cavities (nose, mouth, vagina) and tubular systems (respiratory and gastrointestinal) that produces mucus.

**Mucus**—Slippery liquid produced by the lining of internal cavities and tubular systems to protect tissue.

**Muscle**—Tissue that contracts, often with considerable force, when stimulated by the motor-nerve impulses.

**Muscle Relaxants**—Medications that relieve muscle spasms. They also can have significant side effects.

**Muscle Tumors**—Benign or cancerous tumors arising from muscle tissue.

**Musculo-skeletal System**—The system of bones, muscles, ligaments and tendons that enable the body to move.

**Myelogram, Myelography**—Special x-ray of the spinal canal and spinal cord, requiring a spinal tap and injection of dye that is visible on x-ray film. Myelograms frequently are used to identify the location of ruptured disks.

**Myoma**—Tumor of the muscle.

**Myopia**—Disease of the eye in which close objects are clearly visible while distant objects are blurred. Also called nearsightedness.

**Myringotomy**—A surgical opening made through the eardrum to allow drainage of the middle ear cavity. It is usually performed on children.

**Myxedema Coma**—A life-threatening coma caused by severe hypothyroidism and which can be precipitated by exposure to cold, illness, trauma, infection or sedatives.

# N

**Narcotics**—Medications used to control severe pain. Narcotics should be used only when necessary because of their serious side effects: addiction, reduced breathing, nausea and vomiting, low blood pressure, reduced cough reflex, and constipation.

**Nasogastric Tube**—Slender tube passed through the nose into the stomach. It is used to drain away stomach secretions or to feed patients unable to eat normally.

**Natural Childbirth**—A system of managing childbirth in which the mother receives preparatory education in order to remain conscious during and assist in delivery with minimal or no use of drug or anesthetics.

**Natural Family Planning**—A method of birth control that involves abstinence from sexual intercourse during the period of a woman's ovulation, as determined by observation and measurement of her bodily signs such as temperature and cervical mucus.

**Naturopathy**—Health-care system relying on diet, sunshine, exercises, herbs and other nonmedicinal treatment.

**Nausea**—Unpleasant sensation of being about to vomit.

**Nearsightedness**—See *Myopia*.

**Nebulizer**—Device for administering medications used to treat asthma and similar conditions. It converts medication into a fine mist that is inhaled deeply into the lungs.

**Necrosis**—Death of living tissue as a result of local injury such as loss of blood supply, corrosion, burning or the local lesion of a disease.

**Nerve Block Local Anesthesia**—See *Anesthesia, Local (Nerve Block)*.

**Nerve-Conduction Test**—Diagnostic test that measures the rate at which an electrical impulse moves along a nerve. It is used to diagnose disorders of the peripheral nerves and muscle.

**Nervous Breakdown**—Nontechnical term for mental illness serious enough to interfere with daily activities.

**Neuralgia**—Severe, sharp pain along a nerve.

**Neuritis**—Inflammation of a nerve.

**Neurological**—Relating to the body's nervous system.

**Neurologist**—Doctor specially trained to diagnose and treat diseases of the nervous system.

**Neuro-muscular System**—Nerves and muscles acting together as a system to control body movements.

**Neuroma**—Tumor arising from nerve tissue.

**Neurosis**—Mental illness in which anxiety is controlled by avoidance, blaming others, developing bodily complaints or other mechanisms.

**Neurosurgeon**—Doctor specially trained to diagnose and surgically treat diseases of the brain, spinal cord and nerves.

**Nipple**—1) The small protuberance on a breast through which, in a female, the milk is drawn by a nursing child. 2) An artificial teat through which a bottle-fed child nurses.

**Nodes**—See *Lymph Glands*.

**Nodule**—Small, rounded lump or firm swelling underneath the skin.

**Nonsteroidal Anti-inflammatory Drugs (NSAIDs)**—Medications that control inflammation other than that caused by infection. Usually used to treat conditions of the joints and muscles and pain such as menstrual cramps or headache. "Non-steroidal" means they are not steroid hormones such as cortisone, prednisone, dexamethasone and others.

**Norwalk Virus**—A type of virus that commonly causes epidemics of acute gastroenteritis with diarrhea and vomiting that lasts from 24 to 48 hours.

**NSAIDs**—See *Nonsteroidal Anti-inflammatory Drugs*.

**Nuclear Imaging**—See *Radionuclide Scan*.

**Nurse Practitioner (NP)**—Registered nurse with additional medical training who can diagnose and treat common illness. Nurse practitioners usually work closely with a doctor, although in some states the practitioner can prescribe medicine and work independently of a physician.

**Nutrient**—Food or material containing elements needed to promote growth and development or to support life.

# O

**OB-GYN**—See *Obstetrician-Gynecologist*.

**Obsessions**—Unpleasant, frightening, senseless thoughts that won't go away despite reasoning.

**Obstetrician-Gynecologist**—A physician who has received specialized training in the treatment of diseases of the female reproductive system and the care of pregnant women.

**Occlusion**—Closing or obstruction.

Usually used to describe blockage in blood vessels. In dentistry, it means the way the teeth come together when the mouth is closed.

**Occupational Therapy**—Treatment for people disabled by accident or illness to relearn muscular control and coordination to cope with daily living tasks (dressing, eating, bathing, etc.) and if possible, to resume some form of employment.

**Oncologist**—Doctor specially trained to diagnose and treat cancer.

**Operative Death Rate**—Percentage of patients who die as a result of a certain surgery. It provides general measure of the risk of a surgery.

**Ophthalmologist**—Doctor specially trained to diagnose and treat diseases of the eyes.

**Optic Neuritis**—Inflammation of the nerve that conducts vision impulses from the eye to the brain.

**Oral**—Relating to the mouth.

**Oral-Fecal**—See *Fecal-Oral*.

**Oral Sex**—Oral stimulation of the genitals.

**Organic**—Conditions or diseases resulting from change in body organs that can be measured or seen. Organic diseases are distinct from functional diseases in which no change can be observed in an organ that is not functioning normally.

**Organic Psychosis**—Mental illness that results from disease in the brain.

**Orgasm**—The climax of sexual stimulation, accompanied in women by vaginal contractions, and in men by the ejaculation of sperm.

**Orthodontia**—Straightening teeth by applying temporary braces.

**Orthopedic Surgeon (Orthopedist)**— Doctor specially trained to diagnose and treat diseases of the muscles, bones and joints using surgical or mechanical means. A rheumatologist is an internist who diagnoses and treats similar conditions primarily with medications and other nonsurgical means.

**Osteogenesis Imperfecta**—Inherited condition in which the bones are brittle and easily broken.

**Otolaryngologist**—See *Ear, Nose and Throat Specialist*.

**Ovary**—Female sexual gland where eggs mature and ripen for fertilization.

**Ovulation**—Monthly process in which an egg leaves the ovary for possible fertilization by a sperm cell.

**Ovum**—Egg produced by the ovary.

# P

**Pain**—Unpleasant sensation arising from stimulation of sensory nerves located in almost every part of the body. Disease, injury and strenuous activity can all cause pain.

**Palate**—Roof of the mouth, consisting of a bony front portion (hard palate) and a soft back portion (soft palate).

**Palpitations**—Irregular rapid heartbeat, noticeable to the patient.

**Pancreas**—Organ located on the back abdominal wall that produces and secretes digestive juices into the small intestine. It also produces and secretes insulin into the bloodstream to regulate the level of sugar and other nutrients.

**Pap Smear, Papanicolaou Smear**—Test routinely done to screen for cancer of the cervix and uterus in an early and treatable stage.

**Papule**—Small, raised skin lesion. Papules may be red, brown, yellow, white or skin-colored. They may be flat-topped, pointed or dome-shaped.

**Paranoia**—Mental illness in which a person believes that he or she is being talked about or plotted against.

**Parasite**—Organism that lives within, upon or at the expense of another living organism. Human parasites include disease-causing agents such as amoebas or worms that infect the digestive system, or fungi that live on the skin.

**Parasympathetic Nervous System**— System of nerves that controls digestion, heartbeat and relaxation or contraction of small muscles.

**Parathyroid Glands**—Small glands that control calcium levels in the blood and bones. They are located within or next to the thyroid glands at the base of the neck.

**Passive Exercises**—Exercises in which a therapist moves the arms and legs of a patient while the patient relaxes. These exercises keep the joints limber until the patient is able to move without assistance.

**Patency**—Blood vessels or any hollow organs that clog or become blocked are said to lose their patency.

**Paternal**—Pertaining to, related through or inherited from a father.

**Pathogenic**—Disease-producing.

**Pathological**—Relating to an abnormal condition.

**Pathological Examination**—Laboratory study of abnormal tissue to establish or confirm a diagnosis.

**Pediatrician**—Doctor specially trained to care for children and adolescents, especially to foster normal growth and development.

**Pediculicide**—Medication that cures body lice (pediculosis). Usually applied to the skin.

**Pelvic Examination**—Examination of a woman's reproductive organs to diagnose pregnancy or detect diseases.

**Pelvic Inflammatory Disease (PID)**—Inflammation of the female reproductive tract, especially the fallopian tubes; often sexually transmitted.

**Pelvic Ultrasonography**—Examination of a woman's reproductive organs that uses high-frequency sound waves to create an image. It is used to determine the age, size and position of a fetus in the uterus or to diagnose disease of the pelvic organs.

**Pelvis**—Lower part of the trunk of the body.

**Penis**—Male organ used for urination and sexual intercourse.

**Perforation**—Abnormal hole or opening.

**Perforation, Intestinal**—Complication of conditions such as ulcers, cancers or injury to the digestive system. When this occurs, intestinal contents enter the abdominal cavity, causing severe inflammation.

**Perfusionist**—Medical professional who controls the heart-lung machine to sustain a patient's life during open-heart and lung-transplant surgery.

**Perinatal**—Occurring in or pertaining to the period shortly before and after birth.

**Perinatal Death**—Death of an infant or unborn child in the perinatal period, generally after 28 weeks of gestation or within 4 weeks after birth.

**Perinatologist**—Same as *Maternal-Fetal Medicine Specialist*.

**Perineum**—Area between the vulva and anus in females and between the scrotum and anus in males.

**Peripheral Nervous System**—Nerves that connect to all parts of the body and carry information via electrical impulses to and from the brain and spinal cord.

**Peripheral Vascular System**—Network of arteries, veins and lymphatic channels supplying the head, arms and legs.

**Perirectal**—Skin and underlying tissue around the rectum.

**Peristalsis**—Rhythmic movements of hollow muscular organs (such as the intestines) that move contents (such as digestive material) in one direction.

**Peritoneal Cavity**—Space enclosed by the peritoneum.

**Peritoneum**—Very thin, two-layered tissue. One layer lines the outer surface of all the abdominal organs. The other layer lines the abdominal wall.

**Peritonsillar Abscess**—Abscess forming in the back of the throat near the tonsils.

**Pessary**—Small ring-shaped device that is inserted into the vagina to help maintain the uterus in a normal position.

**Phallus**—Penis.

**pH Balance**—Measure of blood's acidity or alkalinity. The pH is controlled by body fluids and electrolytes. Body tissues cannot function normally if the pH varies from a limited range.

**Phenothiazine Drugs**—Medications used to slow and regulate mental-system activity. Usually used to treat anxiety and other mental conditions; also useful in producing sleep.

**Phlebitis**—Inflammation of a vein.

**Phlebotomy**—Removing blood from the blood vessels. This was once believed to cure many diseases; today, it is done to remove blood for diagnostic testing.

**Phobia**—Fear that cannot be overcome by reason.

**Photochemotherapy**—A treatment for some skin disorders that combines oral medication with exposure to ultraviolet light rays for set periods of time.

**Physical Therapy**—Treatment of diseases of the bone, muscular and nervous systems to help restore normal function after disease or injury.

**Physician's Assistant (PA)**—Someone

trained to do some of the simpler tasks ordinarily performed by a doctor. The PA works under the direction of the doctor.

**Pilocarpine**—Medication used principally in eye drops to treat glaucoma.

**Pituitary Gland**—Small endocrine gland at the base of the brain that controls growth and regulates other endocrine glands.

**Placenta**—Disk-shaped organ that attaches and grows inside the uterus during pregnancy. It enables the fetus to receive nutrients from and transfer natural wastes to the mother's bloodstream. The umbilical cord connects the placenta to the fetus.

**Placenta Accreta**—An abnormal adherence of part or all of the placenta to the uterine wall.

**Placenta Previa**—An abnormal placement of the placenta in the lower uterine segment, so that it covers or adjoins the internal opening of the uterine cervix.

**Plaque**—1) Small raised area of abnormal material on a surface such as the skin or lining of a blood vessel. 2) Mixture of bacteria and calcium deposited on the teeth that can cause cavities and gum diseases.

**Plasma**—Liquid part of blood that remains when blood cells are removed.

**Plastic and Reconstructive Surgeon (Plastic Surgeon)**—Doctor specially trained to perform plastic and reconstructive surgery.

**Plastic and Reconstructive Surgery**—Special surgery to repair and change body parts to improve function or appearance. The face, hands, breasts and skin are areas most frequently treated.

**Platelet Count**—Platelets are blood cells (much smaller than red or white blood cells) that assist in the blood clotting process. A drop of blood contains about 12.5 million platelets. A platelet count determines if the number of platelets is normal.

**Plethysmography**—A study that estimates the amount of blood flowing in vessels by measuring changes in the size of a body part.

**Pleura**—Thin tissue lining the lungs and chest cavity. Inflammation of the pleura (pleurisy) is a painful condition caused by lung diseases.

**Pleural Effusion (Pleural Fluid Effusion)**—Fluid that collects around the lungs, usually caused by inflammation of the lungs and pleura or congestive-heart failure.

**PMS**—See *Premenstrual Syndrome*.

**Podiatrist**—Health-care professional trained in the medical and surgical treatment of foot diseases.

**Polyp**—A growth, often on a stalk arising from dry mucous membranes, such as in the nose, cervix or colon.

**Portal-Vein System**—Veins that drain blood from the gastrointestinal system. The smaller veins empty into the portal vein, which transports blood into the liver.

**Post Coital Test (PCT)**—A study of the cervical mucus performed 2 to 12 hours after intercourse, often as a method of diagnosing cause of infertility in women.

**Postmature Infant**—Infant that spends 3 weeks or more beyond the normal 39 weeks of pregnancy in the womb.

**Postoperative**—Period of recuperation and return to normal health after surgery.

**Postural Drainage**—Exercises and body positions that promote drainage of fluid and secretions that collect in the lungs and airways.

**Potassium**—Electrolyte present in all body cells, blood and body fluids. Potassium is important in maintaining normal heart contractions and the strength and contractions of all muscles. Foods high in potassium include dried apricots and peaches, whole-grain cereals, plain cocoa, dried lentils and peas, bananas and molasses.

**Precancerous**—Characteristic of a growth that has the potential to become cancerous.

**Predisposition**—Tendency. For example, a person who gets many infections has a predisposition to infection.

**Pre-eclampsia**—A toxic condition of late pregnancy characterized by a sudden rise in blood pressure, excessive weight gain, generalized edema, protein in the urine, severe headache and visual disturbances.

**Pregnancy**—The condition, quality or period of being pregnant.

**Premature Delivery**—Delivery of an infant after the 28th week but before completion of the 37th week of gestation.

**Premature Ejaculation**—Male orgasm and ejaculation of sperm following brief sexual stimulation and prior to satisfactory arousal and orgasm in the sexual partner.

**Premature Infant**—An infant born after a gestation period of less than 37 weeks.

**Premature Labor**—Labor occurring prior to the completion of 37 weeks gestation.

**Premenarchal**—Of, relating to or being in the period of life before the first menstrual period occurs.

**Premenopausal**—Of, relating to or being in the period preceding menopause.

**Premenstrual**—Occurring before menstruation or a menstrual period.

**Premenstrual Syndrome (PMS)**—A group of physical and emotional symptoms that may precede a menstrual period, such as fluid retention, headache, fatigue, depression, irritability, etc.

**Presbyopia**—Form of nearsightedness that normally accompanies aging.

**Primary Disorder**—Basic disease that may result in complications. Diabetes mellitus, for example, is a primary disorder that often causes secondary complications involving the kidneys, blood vessels and eyes.

**Proctoscope, Proctoscopy**—Method of examining the rectum and lower part of the colon with a proctoscope, an optical instrument with a lighted tip.

**Prolapse**—Pushing or falling out of a part or an organ from its normal position.

**Prolapsed (Dropped) Uterus**—Uterus that has moved from its normal position because of loose pelvic muscles and ligaments. In severe cases, it can protrude completely outside the vagina.

**Prophylaxis**—Measures taken to prevent an illness.

**Prophylaxis, Dental**—Regular care (including cleaning) of the teeth and gums that helps prevent tooth decay and gum inflammation.

**Prostaglandins**—Natural substances found in semen, menstrual fluid and many body tissues. They are involved in basic body functions such as inflammation, immune response and activities of the lungs, heart, kidneys, uterus and digestive system.

**Prostate (Prostate Gland)**—Male sex gland located at the base of the urinary bladder. It produces a fluid that is added to sperm to produce semen.

**Prosthesis**—Artificial device used as a substitute for a missing or badly functioning part of the body.

**Prothrombin Time**—Test to measure one of the components of the body's blood clotting mechanism. It is used to diagnose clotting diseases and to control blood thinning (anticoagulation) in treatment of some diseases of the heart and blood vessels.

**Protozoa**—One-celled organisms, the smallest type of animal life. Amoeba are protozoa. Some protozoa can cause disease.

**Psychiatrist**—Doctor specially trained to diagnose and treat mental illnesses.

**Psychoanalysis**—Treatment of some mental illness that involves a detailed understanding of how past events in a person's life may have resulted in mental disturbances.

**Psychogenic**—A symptom with an emotional origin instead of an organic one.

**Psychologist**—Health-care professional specially trained to diagnose and treat some kinds of mental illness.

**Psychopathy**—Psychological or mental illness.

**Psychosis**—Mental illness characterized by deranged personality, loss of contact with reality and possible delusions, hallucinations or illusions.

**Psychosocial**—Influences of society on growth and development.

**Psychosomatic Illness**—Illness in which thoughts and emotions play an important role.

**Psychotherapist**—Professional specially trained to diagnose and treat some mental illnesses.

**Puberty**—Period in early adolescence when hormonal changes bring about full sexual maturity and capacity to reproduce.

**Pubic Bone**—One of the bones of the pelvis located above the genitals in both sexes.

**Pubic Lice**—Same as *Crabs*.

**Pulmonary**—Relating to the lungs and breathing.

**Pulmonary Hypertension**—Increased pressure in the blood vessels of the lungs.

**Pulse**—Heartbeat (contraction of the heart) as felt in an artery. Heart rate is often measured by counting the pulse felt in the artery in the wrist.

**Punch Biopsy**—Biopsy which is performed by indenting, perforating or excising a disk or segment of tissue using an instrument known as a punch.

**Pus**—Thick fluid, usually green or yellow, that forms to fight local infection. Pus often collects in an enclosed sac, an abscess, at the site of an infection.

**PUVA**—A type of phototherapy used to treat some skin conditions. It combines the use of a psoralen drug that sensitizes the skin to sunlight with a controlled dose of ultraviolet light.

**Pyelogram, Intravenous**—Method of studying the kidneys and urinary tract by injecting into the bloodstream a medication that x-rays can detect.

**Pyelogram, Retrograde**—Method of studying the kidneys, similar to an intravenous pyelogram, but in which the medication detected by x-rays is placed in the urinary system by a catheter inserted through the bladder into the ureters.

# R

**Radiation Therapy or Treatment**—Use of high-energy waves (generated by special x-ray machines, cobalt machines and other devices) to treat some forms of cancer. Radiation destroys cancerous tissue but does little harm to healthy tissue.

**Radioactive Chromium Studies**—Diagnostic method used to measure total blood in the body.

**Radioactive Iodine Uptake and Scan**—Same as *Thyroid Scan*.

**Radioactive Studies**—Same as *Radioisotope Studies*.

**Radioactive Technetium 99 Scan**—Radioisotope scan method used to diagnose some disorders of the heart, liver, spleen and other organs.

**Radioisotope**—Radioactive form of chemicals normally present in the body.

**Radioisotope Scan**—Scan of radioisotopes given orally or intravenously to a patient that become concentrated in organs such as the heart, lungs or brain. Instruments measure the radiation given off by the radioisotopes and create a photographic image of the organ being studied.

**Radioisotope Studies**—Radioisotopes are chemical elements that give off radiation. A radioisotope of a chemical element normally present in the body (such as carbon), if injected into the body, will mix with the nonisotopes. The body doesn't know the difference, but radiation from the isotopes can be detected with special instruments. Determining where radioisotopes go in the body allows diagnosis of diseases that cannot be detected otherwise.

**Radioisotope Therapy**—Treatment of some cancers with radioisotopes.

**Radiologist**—Doctor specially trained to use x-rays and other kinds of radiation in diagnosis and treatment.

**Radionuclide Scan**—Method of studying various body functions by means of photographs or videotape taken by a special camera or a scanner after intravenous injection of radioactive chemical.

**Rebound Phenomenon**—A reversed response to the withdrawal of a stimulus. A common rebound phenomenon occurs when nose drops, which decrease congestion, wear off. The nasal congestion that develops on the rebound is greater than that which existed before the drops were administered.

**Recovery Room**—Specially equipped and staffed area of a hospital for observing and caring for a patient who has just undergone surgery. Postoperative patients usually remain in the recovery room until they are awake and their vital signs (blood pressure, pulse and respiration) are satisfactory.

**Rectum**—End of the large intestine, located in the pelvis below the sigmoid colon and above the anus.

**Regenerate**—Ability of some parts of the body to grow back to normal after being damaged.

**Regurgitate**—To vomit.

**Relapse**—Stage of illness in which the patient gets worse after having improved.

**Remission**—Stage of a chronic illness when the patient's condition improves.

**Renal**—Having to do with the kidneys.

**Renal Dialysis**—Mechanical and chemical method of removing normal wastes from the body of a patient whose kidneys cannot function adequately. It is also used to remove harmful poison or a drug overdose from the bloodstream.

**Reproductive Organs, Female**—Organs of a woman's body that enable her to become pregnant and deliver a baby. The major organs are the vagina, uterus, fallopian tubes and ovaries.

**Reproductive Organs, Male**—Organs of a man's body that enable him to produce sperm and impregnate a woman. The major organs are the penis, testicles, seminal vesicles and prostate gland.

**Reproductive System**—Body system enabling impregnation and delivery of a baby. It also provides characteristic male or female appearance.

**Resect**—Surgical removal of a part of the body.

**Respiratory-Distress Syndrome**—A condition of newborn infants (often born prematurely) in which the lungs cannot supply adequate oxygen to the body.

**Retained Placenta**—Condition occurring immediately after childbirth in which part of the placenta remains attached to the uterus, creating a risk of serious bleeding or infection.

**Retina**—Light-sensitive part of the eye at the back of the eyeball on which the lens focuses images. The retina converts the image to impulses that go to the brain.

**Retinal-Vein Occlusion**—Condition in which a clot forms in the vein supplying the retina with blood.

**Retinoblastoma**—Cancerous tumor that forms in the eye of an infant.

**Retrograde Pyelography**—See *Pyelogram, Retrograde*.

**Retrovirus**—Group of viruses that cause HIV (human immunodeficiency virus) and some types of lymphoma and leukemia.

**Rheumatologist**—A specialist in internal medicine who subspecializes in medical diagnosis and treatment of rheumatic and arthritic disorders.

**Rhinitis**—Swelling of the nasal passages.

**Rh Negative Blood**—A subtype of red blood cells. Blood subtypes are inherited. The major subtypes are types A, B, O and Rh negative.

**Rhythm Method**—A method of contraception based on the avoidance of sexual intercourse during the time span of a woman's menstrual cycle when ovulation is occurring.

**Rinne Test**—Test using a tuning fork to diagnose hearing disorders.

**Rotavirus**—A type of virus that is often responsible for acute gastroenteritis in infants and diarrhea in young children.

**Rubin's Insufflation Test**—Test used in diagnosing fertility problems in women. A harmless gas is introduced into the uterus to determine if there is a blockage in the fallopian tubes.

## S

**Sacroiliac Region**—Area of the lower back where the spine meets the pelvic bone.

**Saline**—Salt-containing solution similar to normal body fluid that is given intravenously to help correct fluid and electrolyte imbalances.

**Salivary Glands**—Glands located inside the mouth around the jaw that secrete saliva into the mouth.

**Salpingectomy**—Surgical excision of a fallopian tube.

**Salpingitis**—Inflammation of a fallopian tube.

**Salpingolysis**—Surgical correction of adhesions in a fallopian tube.

**Salpingo-Oophorectomy**—Surgical excision of a fallopian tube and an ovary.

**Salpingo-Oophoritis**—Inflammation of a fallopian tube and an ovary.

**Salpingoplasty**—Plastic surgery of a fallopian tube.

**Salpingostomy**—Surgical formation of an opening in a fallopian tube.

**Saphenous-Femoral Vein System**—Network of large veins in the legs that helps return blood from the leg to the inferior vena cava, then to the heart.

**Scale, Scaling**—Flakes of dried skin that form as whitish skin lesions.

**Schizophrenia**—Mental illness characterized by a distorted sense of reality, bizarre behavior and fragmentation of the personality.

**Sciatica**—Painful condition resulting from irritation of the sciatic nerve.

**Sciatic Nerve**—Large nerve that begins at the base of the spine and passes through the buttocks down the back side of the thigh and down the leg.

**Scleritis**—Inflammation of the sclera (the white of the eye).

**Scopolamine**—Medication used to treat hyperactive or spastic conditions of the digestive system and to prevent motion sickness.

**Scrotum**—Organ of the male reproductive system that contains the testicles, blood vessels and the vas deferens.

**Scurvy**—Disease of bones, gums and blood vessels that is caused by a deficiency of vitamin C.

**Secondary Infection**—Infection that results from some other problem. It may occur after surgery or develop during antibiotic treatment of another infection.

**Second Molars**—Permanent grinding teeth that appear at about age 11 to 13.

**Sedative**—Medication used to produce relaxation or sleep.

**Sedative-Hypnotics**—Class of medications that help relieve anxiety and promote sleep.

**Sedimentation Rate**—Blood test measuring the rate that blood settles in a test tube. It identifies infection, inflammation or tissue damage.

**Self-Care**—Treatment that patients can administer for themselves.

**Seminal Vesicles**—Small sacs next to the prostate that help make and store seminal fluid and contract to eject semen.

**Senile Dementia**—Permanent loss of mental functions of older persons, resulting from conditions such as Alzheimer's disease and atherosclerosis (hardening of the arteries).

**Sensate-Focus Exercises**—Exercises in which each partner caresses the other's body without intercourse to learn the relaxed, pleasurable aspects of touching; often used in the treatment of sexual dysfunction.

**Sensitivity Studies (Antibiotics)**—Laboratory method of determining which antibiotic will most likely be successful in treating infections caused by bacteria.

**Sensory**—Ability to feel or experience sensations such as sound, light or pain.

**Septic**—Infected.

**Serological Tests**—Tests of serum (blood without cells) used to diagnose a variety of diseases, especially infections and autoimmune conditions.

**Serum**—Liquid portion of blood that remains after blood cells and blood clots have been removed.

**Serum Alkaline Phosphatase**—Material present in excessive amounts in the blood of patients with some bone and liver diseases.

**Serum Electrolytes**—Same as *Electrolytes*.

**Sesamoid Bones**—Small oval-shaped bones in the tendons of the hands and feet.

**Sever's Disease**—Painful condition of the heel bone of growing children.

**Sexual**—1) Of, relating to or associated with sex or the sexes. 2) Having or involving sex.

**Sexual Abuse**—The act of violating sexually; rape or indecent assault.

**Sexual Dysfunction**—Inability to participate in sexual relations that are satisfactory for both partners.

**Sexual Intercourse**—1) Heterosexual intercourse involving penetration of the vagina by the penis. 2) Intercourse involving genital contact between individuals other than penetration of the vagina by the penis.

**Sexuality**—The quality or state of being sexual. Also, the condition of having sex.

**Sexually Transmitted Disease (STD)**—Any of a variety of diseases transmitted by direct sexual contact or sometimes contracted by other than sexual means; includes the classic venereal diseases such as syphilis, gonorrhea and chancroid, and other diseases such as hepatitis A, hepatitis B and AIDS.

**Shave Biopsy**—Procedure to diagnose skin disorders in which a thin layer of tissue from under a skin lesion is shaved away for laboratory examination.

**Shock**—Condition in which the blood pressure falls below the level needed to supply blood to the body. Signs and symptoms include weakness, paleness, rapid heartbeat, dry mouth, cold sweat and feelings of doom.

**Sick-Sinus Syndrome**—Form of heart-rhythm disorder (arrhythmia).

**SIDS**—See *Sudden Infant Death Syndrome*.

**Sigmoid Colon**—Lower part of the large

colon (intestine) located in the pelvis just above the rectum.

**Sigmoidoscope, Sigmoidoscopy**—Same as *Proctoscope, Proctoscopy.*

**Signs**—Evidence of disease that can be observed and measured, in contrast to symptoms, which only patients can experience. For example, blood pressure measurement or red tonsils are signs; headache or nausea are symptoms.

**Silicone**—Artificial compound used by plastic and reconstructive surgeons to reshape parts of the body, such as the breast.

**Silver Nitrate**—Chemical used for cautery.

**Sims-Huhner Test**—Test used in diagnosis of reasons for infertility in women, in which the mucus from the cervix is examined, especially for presence of sperm after sexual intercourse.

**Skin Clips**—Small U-shaped metal strips used instead of stitches to close skin that has been incised during surgery.

**Skin Tests for Allergy**—Diagnostic method used to determine whether a particular substance is causing allergic reactions. The test is carried out by introducing a small amount of the suspected material, such as pollen or dust, under the skin or on the skin. If inflammation results, the patient is allergic to the material.

**Sleep Apnea**—Intermittent cessation of respiration occurring as a sleep disorder.

**Sleep Inducers**—Medications used to produce sleep.

**Sleep-Study Laboratory**—Laboratory where persons are studied with sensitive instruments while asleep. Information from sleep study aids in diagnosis of sleep disorders.

**Slow Viruses**—Group of viruses that infect the brain but do not cause disease until many years afterward.

**Soaks**—Applying moisture—either plain water or water with dissolved medicines—to an inflamed area of the skin.

**Soft Palate**—Fleshy part of the roof of the mouth close to the throat.

**Sonogram, Sonography**—See *Ultrasound.*

**Spasmodic**—Sudden intermittent symptom, or intermittent muscle spasm.

**Spastic, Spasticity**—A description of muscles that are continuously contracting and in a state of excessive tension.

**Speculum**—Instrument used to examine the interior of openings such as the vagina, nose, ear or rectum.

**Sperm**—Male reproductive cells manufactured in testicles and ejaculated in semen.

**Spermicide**—A preparation or substance used to kill sperm. Also called spermatocide.

**Spherocytosis**—Abnormally shaped red blood cells caused by some anemias. These cells are sphere-shaped, in contrast to the doughnut shape of normal red blood cells.

**Spikes, Temperature**—High but brief episodes of fever.

**Spina Bifida**—Congenital (inherited) disorder in which the base of the spine remains open, sometimes exposing the spinal cord and nerves.

**Spinal Anesthesia**—Method to provide anesthesia to the lower body by injecting an anesthetic into the fluid in the space that surrounds the lower spinal cord.

**Spirometry**—Test of lung (pulmonary) function.

**Spleen**—A large organ in the upper abdomen on the left side, located close to the left side of the stomach. It is the largest structure of the lymph system. The spleen causes disintegration of old red blood cells in adults, manufactures red blood cells in the fetus and newborn and serves as an important reservoir of blood.

**Splenic-Vein Thrombosis**—Clot in the major vein that carries blood away from the spleen.

**Splints**—Rigid supports, made of metal, plastic or plaster, used to immobilize an injured or inflamed part of the body. Splints are used temporarily in the case of injury, following some surgical procedures on joints or ligaments or occasionally in the case of arthritis.

**Spore**—Microscopic seed form of fungi. Spores are extremely hardy and survive extremes of temperature. If they enter the body of a susceptible person, they can cause fungal disease.

**Spotting**—Sporadic bleeding in small

amounts from the uterus, cervix or vagina.

**Sputum**—Secretion of the lungs, coughed up in large amounts in some lung diseases.

**Staphylococcus**—Bacteria that frequently cause boils, abscesses, pneumonias, bone infections and infections in other tissues or organs.

**Staples**—Small U-shaped metal wires used in place of stitches to close incised skin after some surgeries, especially in the digestive system. Also used to close off some portions of the stomach during operations for extreme obesity.

**STD**—See *Sexually Transmitted Disease*.

**Stenosis**—Constriction or narrowing of a passage or opening.

**Sterility**—Incapability of producing offspring.

**Sterilized**—1) Made completely free of all germs, usually by steam heat, toxic gas or chemicals. All instruments used in surgeries are sterilized, as is most other medical equipment. 2) Made unable to conceive children.

**Steroids**—Medications that resemble hormones produced by the cortex of the adrenal glands, ovaries and testicles.

**Stethoscope**—Instrument used to listen to the sounds produced by the heart, lungs, blood vessels and pregnant uterus.

**Still's Disease**—Form of arthritis in children similar to rheumatoid arthritis in adults.

**Stimulant Drugs**—Medications that increase the activity of the brain and nervous system.

**Stomatitis**—Inflammation of the mouth.

**Stool**—Feces.

**Streptococcus**—Bacteria that cause illnesses such as laryngitis, cellulitis of the skin, pneumonia, meningitis and others. If not treated, streptococcal infections may also cause serious heart and kidney diseases as complications that appear after the original infection has cleared.

**Stricture**—Abnormal narrowing of a bodily passage (as from inflammation, cancer or the formation of a scar).

**Subcutaneous**—Under the skin.

**Sublingual Salivary Glands**—Small glands near the base of the tongue that secrete saliva into the mouth.

**Submaxillary Salivary Glands**—Small glands near the jaw that secrete saliva into the mouth.

**Sudden Infant Death Syndrome (SIDS)**—Death of an apparently healthy infant, usually before one year of age, that is of unknown cause and occurs usually during sleep. Also called crib death.

**Sulfonamides (Sulfa Drugs)**—Class of drugs used to fight infections.

**Sulfonurea Drugs**—Medications taken orally to treat some forms of diabetes mellitus.

**Surgery**—Treatment in which the body is restored to a healthy condition by physical methods (or operations) such as cutting, removing, replacing, straightening, repairing or joining.

**Surgical Suite**—Group of rooms used to perform surgery. In addition to operating rooms, where surgery takes place, there are supply areas, a recovery room, administrative rooms and a lounge for the staff to rest between surgeries.

**Surrogate Mother**—A mother who contracts to bear a child for another woman who is sterile. The pregnancy is achieved through artificial insemination with sperm, often from the male partner of the sterile woman. The egg may be from the surrogate mother, or from another donor. The surrogate mother agrees to turn the baby over for adoption right after birth.

**Suture**—Thread-like material used to hold tissues or skin edges together.

**Symmetry, Symmetrical**—Refers to the arrangement of the body in pairs, such as two arms, legs, kidneys, lungs, etc.

**Sympathomimetics**—Medications similar to adrenalin in their actions.

**Symptoms**—Effects of disease that only the patient can experience, such as pain, nausea, dizziness, anxiety, depression and others.

**Syndrome**—A group of signs and symptoms that occur together and characterize a particular abnormality.

**Synovial Membranes**—Delicate tissue that lines the inside of joints.

**Systemic**—Conditions that affect most or all of the body, in contrast to conditions that affect only a limited area. For example, diabetes mellitus is a systemic condition; an abscess is a local condition.

# T

**Tartar**—Hard deposit that forms on the teeth and causes inflammation of the gums.

**Temperature Spike**—See *Spikes, Temperature*.

**Temporomandibular Joint**—Joint that joins the jaw to the other head bones.

**Tenderness**—Condition that causes pain when pressure is applied.

**Tendon**—Tough cord of tissue at the end of muscles that attach to bone. Tendons transmit the force of muscle contraction to cause movement.

**TENS**— See *Transcutaneous Electric Nerve Stimulation*.

**Testes or Testicles**—Male sex glands that produce sex hormones and sperm.

**Test Tube Baby**—A baby conceived by in-vitro fertilization.

**Therapeutic Trial**—Form of diagnosis and treatment in which medication is used even though the diagnosis is not firmly established. If the patient improves after treatment with a medication known to be useful in treating a specific condition, the improvement suggests that the specific disease was present. Therapeutic trials are somewhat risky and are used only when other forms of diagnosis and treatment have failed.

**Therapist**—Health-care professional specially trained to provide therapy.

**Thermogram, Thermography**—Method of diagnosis that measures body heat. The area being studied is scanned by a heat-sensitive instrument capable of producing an image (thermogram) of areas of increased heat. They are useful in studying female breast tumors and some blood vessel conditions.

**Thiazide Diuretics**—Class of medications that promote excretion of excess fluids by the kidneys.

**Third Molars**—Permanent grinding teeth that appear at about age 17 to 25.

**Thoracic Duct**—The largest channel of the lymphatic system, through which lymph fluid enters the vena cava.

**Thoracic Spine**—That part of the spinal column below the neck and above the back. Ribs attach to the thoracic spine.

**Thoracic Surgeon**—A surgeon who specializes in surgical treatment of disorders of the organs in the thorax (chest), including lungs, pericardium, heart, pleura (covering of lungs), bronchial tubes and large blood vessels.

**Thrombophlebitis**—Inflammation of a vein caused by a clot that forms within the blood vessel and remains attached to its place of origin.

**Thyroglossal Duct**—Small passageway, normally closed, located in the upper neck. It extends from the back of the tongue to just above the larynx. If an abnormally open duct becomes filled with fluid, a thyroglossal cyst results.

**Thyroid Cartilage**—Larynx (also called the voice box, or Adam's apple), made of semi-hard cartilage.

**Thyroid Gland**—Endocrine gland located in the lower neck next to the trachea that produces hormones that regulate the rate at which all body cells function. Thyroid hormones are also essential for normal growth and development.

**Thyroid Scan**—Method of examination of the thyroid gland in which a small amount of radioactive iodine introduced into the body collects in the thyroid gland. An instrument passed over the thyroid produces an image of the gland based on the concentration of the radioactive iodine.

**Ticks**—Small biting insects that may cause inflammation of the skin or serious infections such as Rocky Mountain spotted fever.

**Tics**—Brief, uncontrollable muscle spasms. Tics usually involve the face and the shoulders.

**Tissue**—Building blocks of body organs; living cells all of one type.

**Tonsils**—Lymphatic tissues that help fight infection located at the entrance of the throat. They frequently become infected, especially in children.

**Topical**—Medications applied to the skin, conjunctiva, or mucous membrane of the mouth, nose, vagina or rectum.

**Tourette's Syndrome**—A rare disorder of movement. It involves repetitive grimaces and tics, usually of the head and neck, sometimes arms, legs and trunk. Involuntary noises and foul language may occur.

**Tourniquet**—Cord or band wrapped around an arm or leg tightly enough to stop blood circulation temporarily.

**Toxic, Toxicity**—Harmful; capable of causing body damage.

**Toxin**—Poison. Usually refers to the chemicals produced by some living organisms that harm the human body.

**Traction**—Method of treating some conditions of bones, muscles and ligaments by exerting a steady pull on the affected parts. Some bone fractures and back pain due to a ruptured disk are treated this way.

**Tranquilizer**—Medication used to help diminish anxiety and to produce calmness.

**Tranquilizers, Benzodiazepine**—Class of tranquilizers commonly used to treat anxiety, nervousness or tension.

**Transcutaneous Electric Nerve Stimulation (TENS)**—A pocket-size device that can suppress certain types of pain by the application of weak electrical current to the affected area.

**Transfuse**—To give a patient blood, necessary in treatment of some conditions.

**Transfusion**—Process of introducing blood through a needle placed in the patient's vein.

**Transfusion Reaction**—Undesirable symptom or condition resulting from a blood transfusion.

**Transmission, Transmit**—Passing a disease to another person.

**Transplant, Transplantation**—Living organ (such as kidney, cornea, heart, bone marrow or skin) removed from one person (donor) and placed in the body of another (recipient).

**Transverse Colon**—Middle part of the colon (intestine), lying horizontally in the middle or upper abdomen.

**Trauma**—Force that injures or damages any part of the body.

**Tricyclic Antidepressant Drugs (Tricyclics)**—Class of medications used to treat depression.

**Trophoblastic Tumors**—See *Hydatidiform Mole.*

**Tubal Ligation**—A method of sterilization in which the fallopian tubes are blocked in such a way that the ovum becomes inaccessible for fertilization.

**Tube Feeding**—Providing nutrients through a small tube placed in the stomach of patients who are unable to eat. The tube may pass through the nose to the stomach or be inserted through an incision in the stomach.

**Tuberous Sclerosis**—Rare inherited condition of the skin, nervous system and other organs of the body.

**Tumor**—Literally, a swelling; usually used to refer to a benign or cancerous growth.

# U

**Ulceration**—Wearing away of the surface or lining of an organ, exposing underlying tissue. Ulceration of the lining of the stomach exposes blood vessels, which may bleed. Ulceration may erode through the wall of an organ (perforation). Ulceration frequently affects the skin, if rubbed excessively or if diseased.

**Ultrasonography**—Diagnostic method in which high-frequency (ultrasound) sound waves are transmitted into the body. Their reflections create images of body organs.

**Ultrasound Treatment**—Method of treatment in which high-energy sound waves are focused on the affected area, producing mild heat that helps relieve inflammation. It is especially useful in treatment of muscular symptoms.

**Underlying**—Beneath, below or more basic. Thus, losing weight may result from an underlying condition such as diabetes mellitus or cancer.

**Upper Gastrointestinal Series (Upper GI Series)**—X-ray examination of the esophagus, stomach and duodenum accomplished by having the patient swallow barium solution that x-rays can detect.

**Upper Respiratory System**—Upper part of the breathing system, consisting of the nose, throat, larynx, trachea and bronchial tubes.

**Uremia**—A serious condition associated with kidney failure in which body wastes build up in the blood and body tissues.

**Ureters**—Slender muscular tubes that carry urine from the kidneys to the urinary bladder, where it is stored until eliminated from the body.

**Urethra**—Tubular passageway extending

from the urinary bladder to the outside of the body.

**Urethritis**—Inflammation of the urethra.

**Urethroscope**—An instrument for viewing the interior of the urethra.

**Urethroscopy**—Examination of the urethra by means of a urethroscope.

**Urethrostomy**—The creation of a surgical opening between the perineum and the urethra.

**Urethrotomy**—Surgical incision into the urethra, especially for the relief of stricture.

**Urethrovaginal**—Of, relating to or adjoining the urethra and vagina.

**Urgency**—A compelling desire to urinate or defecate due to some abnormal stress (inflammation or infection).

**Uric Acid**—Chemical normally produced in the body from metabolism or breakdown of protein and eliminated in the urine. If the level of uric acid rises in the body as a result of disease, gout or kidney stones may result.

**Urinalysis**—Laboratory test performed on a urine sample that helps diagnose diseases of the kidney and other parts of the body.

**Urinary Bladder**—Muscular sac in the lower abdomen that stores urine brought to it from the kidneys by the ureters. The bladder stores urine until it can be eliminated through the urethra by contractions of the bladder muscles.

**Urinary Studies**—Laboratory or x-ray tests of the urinary tract.

**Urinary Tract**—Organs that produce, store and eliminate urine. The organs are the kidneys, ureters, urinary bladder and urethra.

**Urination**—The act of urinating.

**Urine**—A waste material that is excreted by the kidneys and is usually clear, amber and slightly acidic.

**Urography**—See *Intravenous Urography*.

**Uterus**—Organ of the female reproductive system on the wall of which the fertilized egg (ovum) attaches and develops to form a fetus.

**Uveitis**—Inflammation of the parts of the eyes that make up the iris (the colored tissue encircling the clear center, the pupil).

**Uvula**—Soft tissue hanging down from the soft palate at the back of the throat.

# V

**Vaccination**—Method of providing protection against disease (immunity) by giving a patient a small amount of the disease-causing germ that is weakened, killed or otherwise modified so that it cannot itself cause disease. Same as *Immunization*.

**Vaccine**—Medication used to provide immunity by vaccination. Vaccines are given mostly by injection or by mouth.

**Vagina**—A canal in the female that leads from the uterus to the external orifice opening.

**Vaginal**—Of, relating to, affecting or resembling a vagina.

**Vaginectomy**—Partial or complete surgical excision of the vagina; also called colpectomy.

**Vagus Nerve**—Long cranial nerve, arising in the base of the brain and passing to the chest and abdomen. It helps regulate heart rate, breathing, swallowing, digestion and many other body functions.

**Varicose**—Swollen and twisting; usually used to describe varicose veins.

**Vasculitis**—Inflammation of blood vessels, the basis of many illnesses.

**Vas Deferens**—Tube that carries sperm manufactured by the testicles toward the prostate gland and seminal vesicles.

**Vasoconstrictor Drugs**—Medications that cause blood vessels to contract, tighten or become smaller.

**Vasodilator Drugs**—Medications that cause small arteries to widen, providing more blood to an area of the body where the blood vessels are constricted by spasm, narrowed or obstructed.

**Vector**—1) An imaginary line that represents both direction and quantity used to study electrocardiograms (ECGs). 2) An agent that transmits infectious germs from one organism to another.

**Veins**—Blood vessels that return blood from body organs to the heart and lungs. Veins are much thinner than arteries. Veins carry blood at a much lower pressure than do arteries.

**Vena Cava**—Largest vein in the body. It collects blood from the venous system and carries it to the heart.

**Vena Cavography**—Method of studying the vena cava by injecting into the bloodstream a medication that x-rays can detect.

**Venereal**—Related to sexual intercourse or sexual contact. Venereal diseases such as genital herpes, gonorrhea or syphilis are now usually referred to as sexually transmitted diseases (STDs).

**Venography**—Method of studying the veins by injecting into the bloodstream a medication that x-rays can detect.

**Venous System**—Network of veins that extend from all body organs and transport blood back to the heart.

**Ventricles**—Chambers containing fluid. The ventricles of the heart pump blood; ventricles of the brain contain cerebrospinal fluid.

**Ventricular Aneurysm**—Ballooning of the wall of the heart resulting from a weakening of the heart muscle, a complication of scarring from a previous heart attack.

**Vertebrae**—Bones of the spine that form the vertebral column (backbone).

**Vertebral Column**—The spine; the bones of the back.

**Virulent**—Extremely dangerous or harmful. Virulent bacteria are ones capable of causing diseases.

**Viruses**—Small germs responsible for a variety of infectious illnesses. Viruses are not alive until they enter cells of the body, where they grow and reproduce, causing viral illnesses.

**Visual Acuity**—Clarity with which objects are seen.

**Vitamins**—Chemical substances found in food that are necessary for healthy body growth, function and tissue repair.

**Vitreous**—Clear fluid that fills much of the eye.

**Vocal Cords**—Two narrow bands of fibrous and muscular tissue in the larynx that vibrate to create the sounds of the voice.

**Volvulus**—Twisting of loops of intestines, which become closed off (obstructed) and may lose their blood supply.

**Vomit**—To disgorge the contents of the stomach through the mouth.

**Vulva**—The external genitalia of the female including the clitoris and vaginal lips.

**Vulvectomy**—Surgical excision of the vulva.

# W

**Warts**—Small, often hard and rough skin growths caused by viruses that infect the skin.

**Wasting of Body or Muscles**—Severe loss of body tissues (other than surplus fat), especially muscles and vital organs, resulting in weakness, susceptibility to infection, bone fractures and sometimes death.

**Weber Test**—Hearing test performed with a tuning fork.

**Wheal**—A temporary skin elevation, usually a result of an allergic reaction.

**Wheezes**—High-pitched sounds and whistles produced in the lungs where secretions have partially blocked air passages.

**Whirlpool Treatment**—Method of treating minor blood vessel and musculo-skeletal diseases by immersion in a pool where jets of warm water enter and swirl under high pressure.

**Wisdom Teeth**—Same as *Third Molars*.

# X

**X-rays**—High-energy, invisible waves capable of penetrating the body and creating shadows on photographic film. The shadows provide images of the body tissues through which the x-rays pass.

**Xeroradiogram**—Method of x-ray diagnosis, usually of the female breast, which uses a process similar to that used to produce photocopies.

**Xerosis**—Abnormal dryness.

# Y

**Yellow Fever**—An acute disease caused by a virus spread by insect bites. Usually seen in Africa and South America.

**Yersinia Infection**—A type of food-borne bacteria that can cause gastroenteritis and diarrhea.

# Z

**Zoster**—Used to describe a form of virus infection (herpes zoster, shingles) that often produces bands of inflammation across the chest or abdomen.

**Zygote**—The fertilized egg before division.

**Zygote Intrafallopian Transfer (ZIFT)**—An alternative to in-vitro fertilization in which fertilized eggs are transferred into a woman's fallopian tubes so that early development occurs in the tube, rather than in the lab.

# Resources for Additional Information
## (Medical Information Self-Help Directory)

Medical self-help groups and other support groups are an important source of additional information for many disorders and other problems or concerns involving women.

These consumer groups can provide you with useful information about disorders and treatments as well as needed emotional support. Most have toll-free numbers that you can call. If you have access to a computer and a modem, on-line sources can also be helpful.

Alcoholics Anonymous
475 Riverside Dr., 11th Floor
New York, NY 10115; (212) 870-3400;
http://www.recovery.org/aa

Alliance of Genetic Support Groups
4301 Connecticut Avenue NW, Suite 404
Washington, DC 20008; (800) 336-GENE;
http://www.geneticalliance.org

Alopecia Areata Foundation
714 C Street, Suite 216
San Rafeal, CA 94901; (415) 456-4644

Alzheimer's Association
(800) 272-3900; http://www.alz.org

American Academy of Pediatrics
P.O. Box 927, Elk Grove Village, IL 60007;
http://www.aap.org

American Cancer Society
1599 Clifton Road, Atlanta, GA 30329;
(800) ACS-2345; http://www.cancer.org

American College of Obstetricians & Gynecologists
409 12th St, Washington, DC 20024-2188;
(202) 638-5577; http://www.acog.com/

American Diabetes Association
P.O. Box 25757, 1660 Duke Street
Alexandria, VA 22314; (800) 232-3472;
http://www.diabetes.org

American Heart Association
(800) AHA-USA-1; http://www.amhrt.org

American Liver Foundation
1425 Pompton Avenue
Cedar Grove, NJ 07009; (800) 223-0179;
http://www.liverfoundation.org

American Lung Association
(800) LUNG-USA; http://www.lungusa.org

American Lupus Society
(800) 331-1802

American Society for Reproductive Medicine
1209 Montgomery Highway
Birmingham, AL 35216; (205) 978-5000;
http://www.asrm.org

American Society of Plastic and
Reconstructive Surgeons
444 East Algonquin Road
Arlington Heights, IL 60005; (800) 635-0635

Anorexia Nervosa & Related Eating Disorders
P.O. Box 5102, Eugene, OR 97405;
(503) 344-1144

Anorexia Nervosa and Associated Disorders
Box 7, Highland Park, IL 60035;
(708) 831-3438

Anxiety Disorders of America
11900 Parklawn Drive, Suite 100
Rockville, MD 20852-2624; (301) 231-9350;
http://www.adaa.org

Arthritis Foundation
(800) 283-7800; http://www.arthritis.org

Asthma & Allergy Foundation of America
1717 Massachusetts Avenue, Suite 305
Washington, DC, 20036 (800) 7AS-THMA;
http://www.housecall.com/sponsors/nhc/
1996vha/aafa

Chronic Fatigue Syndrome & Immune Deficiency Syndrome
P.O. Box 220398, Charlotte, NC 28222;
(800) 442-3437;
http://www.ybi.com/cfids/tcaa.html

Cocaine Abuse Hotline
(800) COCAINE

Daughters of Hirsutism Association
203 North La Salle Street, Suite 2100
Chicago, IL 60601; (312) 558-1365

DES Action USA
1615 Broadway, #510, Oakland, CA 94612

Drug Abuse Clearinghouse
11426 Rockville Pike, Suite 200
Rockville, MD 20852; (301) 443-6500

Endometriosis Association
8585 North 76th Place, Milwaukee, WI 53223;
(800) 992-ENDO;
http://www.ivg.com/endoassn.html

Epilepsy Foundation of America
(800) EFA-1000; http://www.efa.org

Fertility Research Foundation
1430 Second Avenue, Suite 103
New York, NY 10021; (212) 744-5500

Food and Drug Administration (FDA) Breast
Implant Information Hotline
(800) 532-4440

Herpes Resource Center
P.O. Box 13827
Research Triangle Park, NC 27709;
(919) 361-8488

Hysterectomy Educational Resources & Services
(HERS) Foundation
422 Bryn Mawr Avenue
Bala-Cynwyd, PA 19004; (610) 667-7757;
http://www.ccon.com/hers

# Resources for Additional Information
# (Medical Information Self-Help Directory) (cont.)

Impotence Information Center Hotline
(800) 843-4315

Interstitial Cystitis Association
P.O. Box 1553, Madison Square
New York, NY 10159; (800) 422-1626;
http://www.ichelp.com

La Leche League International
(800) LA-LECHE;
http://www.prairienet.org/LLLi/homepage.html

National Abortion Federation
1436 U Street NW, Suite 103
Washington, DC 20009; (800) 772-9100

National AIDS Hotline
(800) 342-AIDS; http://www.cdcnac.org

National Alliance for the Mentally Ill
(800) 950-6264; http://www.nami.org

National Alliance of Breast Cancer Organizations
(NABCO)
9 East 37th Street, 10th Floor
New York, NY 10016; (217) 719-0154

National Association for Continence
P.O. Box 8310, Spartanburg, SC 29305;
(800) BLADDER; http://www.nafc.org

National Breast Cancer Coalition
1707 L Street NW, Suite 1060
Washington, DC 20036; (202) 296-7477;
http://www.natlbcc.org/

National Cancer Institute
(800) 4-CANCER; http://www.nci.nih.gov

National Center for Education in Maternal and
Child Health
2000 15th Street North, Suite 701
Arlington, VA 22201; (703) 524-7802

National Coalition Against Domestic Violence
P.O. Box 18749, Denver, CO 80218-0749;
(303) 839-1852

National Depressive and Manic Depressive
Association
(800) 826-3632

National Domestic Violence Hotline
(800) 799-SAFE;
TTY for the deaf (800) 787-3224;
http://www.inetport.com/~ndvh

National Drug and Alcohol Hotline
(800) 662-4357

National Eating Disorders Organization (NEDO)
Laureate Hospital, 6655 S. Yale Avenue
Tulsa, OK 74136

National Foundation for Mental Illness
(800) 239-1263

National Headache Foundation
(800) 843-2256; http://www.headaches.org

National Heart, Lung and Blood Institute
Communications and Public Information
Branch, National Institute of Health, Bldg 31
Room 41-21, 9000 Rockville Pike
Bethesda, MD 20892

National Institute of Mental Health (NIMH)
National Anxiety Awareness Program
9000 Rockville Pike, Bethesda, MD 20892;
(800) 64-PANIC; http://www.nimh.nih.gov

National Institute on Aging
(800) 222-2225

National Lymphedema Network
2211 Post Street, Suite 404
San Francisco, CA 94115-3427;
(800) 541-3259; http://hooked.net/~lymphnet

National Mental Health Association
(800) 969-6642

National Multiple Sclerosis Society
(800) 344-4867; http://www.nmss.org

National Organization for Rare Disorders
(800) 999-NORD;
http://www.pcnet.com/~orphan

National Osteoporosis Foundation
1150 17th Street, Suite 500 NW
Washington, DC 20036; (800) 223-9994;
http://www.nof.org

National Pediculosis Association
P.O. Box 149, Newton, MA 02161;
(617) 449-NITS

PMS Access
P.O. Box 9326, Madison, WI 53715;
(800) 222-4PMS

Recovery of Male Potency
(800) 835-7667

Sexually Transmitted Diseases Hotline
(800) 227-8922

Society for Menstrual Cycle Research
10559 North 104th Place
Scottsdale, AZ 85258; (602) 451-9731

Y-Me National Organization for Breast Cancer
Information
(800) 221-2141;
http://www.y-me.org/index.html

# Emergency First Aid

## ANAPHYLAXIS (Severe allergic reaction)

**Symptoms**

Itching, rash, hives, runny nose, wheezing, paleness, cold sweats, dizziness, low blood pressure, coma, cardiac arrest. Symptoms usually occur within 30 minutes after an insect sting or ingestion of certain foods or drugs.

**Treatment**

### If Victim Is Unconscious, Not Breathing

1. Yell for help. Don't leave victim.
2. Call or have someone call 911 (or your local emergency number) for an ambulance or medical help.
3. Clear the victim's mouth of foreign material, tilt jaw forward without moving the neck, pinch nose shut, cover victim's mouth with your mouth and begin mouth-to-mouth breathing. Give one slow breath every 5 seconds.
4. If there is no pulse, give cardiopulmonary resuscitation (CPR). Place hands on center of breastbone, press down 15 times and then do rescue breathing, giving 2 slow breaths.
5. Keep alternating between chest compressions and rescue breathing until help arrives or the victim is breathing on his or her own and there is a pulse.

### If Victim Is Unconscious and Breathing

1. Call or have someone call 911 (or your local emergency number) for an ambulance or medical help.
2. If you can't get help immediately, take patient to nearest emergency room or other facility with adequate equipment and personnel to care for medical emergencies.

## BLEEDING

**Symptoms**

Bleeding caused by any serious injury should be treated in an emergency facility. There is usually a lot of bright-red blood pumping from an injured artery, or darker blood if a large vein has been injured.

**Treatment**

1. Call or have someone call 911 (or your local emergency number) for an ambulance or medical help. In the meantime, render first aid yourself.
2. Cover the injured area with the cleanest cloth you can find, or bare hands if no cloth is available.
3. Apply strong pressure directly on injured area with the heel of your hand until the bleeding stops or medical help arrives.
4. If possible, raise a bleeding arm or leg (if not broken) above the level of the victim's heart.

# Emergency First Aid (continued on next page)

## BURNS

### Symptoms

First- and second-degree burns are not usually life-threatening.
First-degree burns cause only red skin and mild swelling.
Second-degree burns cause blisters, pain and oozing.
Third-degree burns can be life-threatening if extensive. Skin turns white or appears charred.

### Treatment for first- and most second-degree burns

1. Place the victim's burned area under cold running water for 15 to 20 minutes. Don't put ice directly on the burn and don't apply butter.
2. Cover the burn area with clean, moist bandages and seek medical assistance.

### Treatment for more extensive burns

1. Keep victim lying flat and lightly covered to prevent shock. Elevate the feet and legs if possible. Wrap or cover the burned area with a clean, moist cloth. Call or have someone call 911 (or your local emergency number) for an ambulance or medical help.
2. Remove clothes and jewelry unless they are sticking to burned skin. Do not immerse the victim in a cold bath or apply any type of ointment.

### Special instructions

Electrical Burns—Turn off the source of electricity if possible. If not, use a non-conductive material, such as a board or wooden chair, to pull the victim away from the electrical source. Don't use your bare hands. If the victim is not breathing, begin mouth-to-mouth breathing.

Chemical Burns of the Eye or Skin—Hold the victim's head or other burned area beneath a faucet. Turn on cool water at medium pressure. Rinse for at least 15 minutes, directing the water away from the unaffected area.

For Burns of Large Areas—Prepare a solution for the victim to drink on the way to the emergency room. Mix 1 quart of water with 1 teaspoon of salt and 1/2 teaspoon of baking soda. This may help prevent kidney failure.

# Emergency First Aid (cont.)

## CHOKING

### Symptoms
Clutching at throat and is unable to speak. Has trouble breathing or is unable to breathe; skin may turn blue, white or gray. Loss of consciousness.

### Treatment
1. If the victim can still talk, breathe and cough, don't intervene.
2. If the victim is unable to breathe, cough and talk, perform the Heimlich Maneuver as follows:

### Heimlich Maneuver
1. Stand behind person, place both arms around his abdomen and clasp your hands just below the ribcage and above the naval. Make a fist with one hand, thumb side in. Grasp the fist with your other hand.
2. Give 3 or 4 quick forceful squeezes, pushing in and up until the object is coughed up.
3. If victim becomes unconscious, call for emergency help. If necessary, perform rescue breathing and CPR as described above until help arrives.

Note: If you are alone and are choking, lean forward on your abdomen against the back of a chair and push forcefully.

## FRACTURES OR DISLOCATIONS

### Symptoms
Extreme pain and tenderness in any injured area; change in appearance of injured part, such as swelling, protruding bone or blood under skin. Extremity, such as finger, arm or leg, may be bent out of normal alignment.

### Treatment
1. Immobilize any injured area and don't move a broken limb unless absolutely necessary. Keep victim as warm and comfortable as possible. Control any bleeding. Call or have someone call 911 (or your local emergency number) for an ambulance or medical help.
2. If you must move a victim, improvise a splint from stiff rolled-up paper, scrap wood or metal. Pad the splint with clothing or blankets. The splint should extend beyond the joint on either end of the injury. Attach splint firmly to injured extremity with strips of cloth, twine or similar material to prevent movement (don't cut off the blood flow).
3. If leg, back or neck is severely injured and possibly fractured or dislocated, keep patient warm and still until ambulance arrives. Don't move the victim.

## HEART ATTACK

### Symptoms

Chest pain lasting more than 10 minutes that radiates into jaw or arm. Heavy sweating without obvious other cause. Weakness, nausea, pale skin. Irregular pulse.

### Treatment

#### If Victim Is Unconscious, Not Breathing

1. Yell for help. Don't leave victim.
2. Call or have someone call 911 (or your local emergency number) for an ambulance or medical help.
3. Clear the victim's mouth of foreign material, tilt jaw forward without moving the neck, pinch nose shut, cover victim's mouth with your mouth and begin mouth-to-mouth breathing. Give one slow breath every 5 seconds.
4. If there is no pulse, give cardiopulmonary resuscitation (CPR). Place hands on center of breastbone, press down 15 times and then do rescue breathing, giving 2 slow breaths.
5. Keep alternating between chest compressions and rescue breathing until help arrives or the victim is breathing on his or her own and there is a pulse.

#### If Victim Is Unconscious and Breathing

1. Call or have someone call 911 (or your local emergency number) for an ambulance or medical help.
2. If you can't get help immediately, take patient to nearest emergency room or other facility with adequate equipment and personnel to care for medical emergencies.

# Index

*An asterisk (\*) in front of an entry denotes the name of a "symptom", which can be found in the Symptoms section beginning on page 1.*

*An asterisk (\*) in front of an entry denotes the name of a "symptom", which can be found in the Symptoms section beginning on page 1.*

*An asterisk (\*) in front of an entry denotes the name of a "symptom", which can be found in the Symptoms section beginning on page 1.*

*An asterisk (\*) in front of an entry denotes the name of a "symptom", which can be found in the Symptoms section beginning on page 1.*

*An asterisk (*) in front of an entry denotes the name of a "symptom", which can be found in the Symptoms section beginning on page 1.*

*An asterisk (\*) in front of an entry denotes the name of a "symptom", which can be found in the Symptoms section beginning on page 1.*

*An asterisk (\*) in front of an entry denotes the name of a "symptom", which can be found in the Symptoms section beginning on page 1.*

* Sexual Intercourse, Painful 34
Sexually Transmitted Diseases 161
Sexually Transmitted Diseases Hotline 381
SGA 250
SIL 85
Sleep Disorders 317
Small-for-Gestational-Age (SGA) Pregnancy 250
Smoking 335
Smoking & Pregnancy 277
Society for Menstrual Cycle Research 381
Soft Chancre 90
Spermicides 188, 199
Sponge (contraception) 188
Spontaneous Abortion 252
Spousal Abuse 307
Squamous Intraepithelial Lesions (SIL) 85
STDs 161
STDs, Condom Usage to Prevent 94
Stein-Leventhal Syndrome 153
Sterilization, surgical 189
Stress 336
Substance Abuse & Addiction 337
Suction Curettage 216
Suction Lipectomy 318
Surgical sterlization 189
* Sweating, Excessive 35
* Swelling, Abdominal 5
* Swelling or Lump 36
Syphilis 162

**T**
Tests, Infertility 288
Thromboembolic Disorders 163
* Tiredness or Fatigue 17
Total Mastectomy 76
Toxemia of Pregnancy 264
Toxic Shock Syndrome 164
Toxoplasmosis 165
* Trembling or Twitching 38
Trichomonal Vaginitis 179

Trichomoniasis 179
Triple Screen 219
Trophoblastic Disease, Gestational 243
TSS 164
Tubal Ligation 189, 200
Tubal or Extrauterine Pregnancy 234
Tummy Tuck 338
Tumor Removal, Fibroid 110
Tumor Removal, Ovarian 146
* Twitching or Trembling 38

**U**
Ultrasound Scanning 340
Unconjugated Estriol Test 219
Urethral Caruncle Removal 166
Urethritis 168
Urethrocele 173
Urinary Tract Infection in Pregnancy 282
* Urination, Frequent 39
* Urination, Lack of Control 41
* Urination, Painful 42
* Urine, Abnormal Color 43
Uterine Biopsy 106
Uterine Bleeding, Dysfunctional 169
Uterine Bleeding, Postmenopausal 170
Uterine Malignancy 171
Uterine Prolapse 172
UTI in Pregnancy 282

**V**
Vaginal Bleeding during Pregnancy 283
* Vaginal Bleeding, Unexpected 44
* Vaginal Discharge, Abnormal 46
Vaginal Hernias 173
* Vaginal Itching 47
Vaginal or Vulvar Cancer 174
Vaginal Yeast Infection 177
Vaginismus 175
Vaginitis, Atrophic 178
Vaginitis, Bacterial 176

*An asterisk (\*) in front of an entry denotes the name of a "symptom", which can be found in the Symptoms section beginning on page 1.*

# OTHER BOOKS OF INTEREST
### From H. Winter Griffith, M.D